SPORT CA
Coloring Book

MW00876876

FOR KIDS 4-12

Copyright ©2021

inkHORSE Publishing

All Rights Reserved

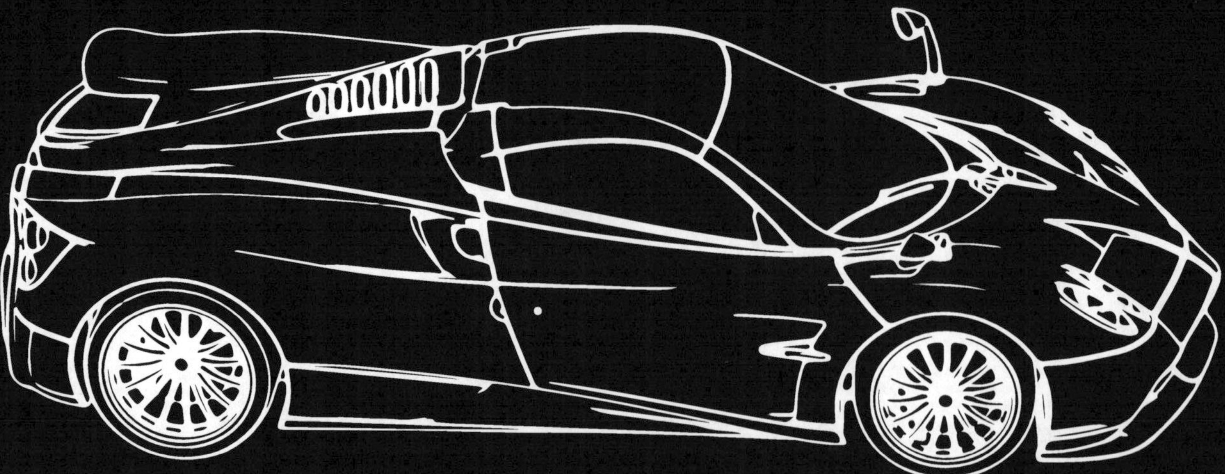

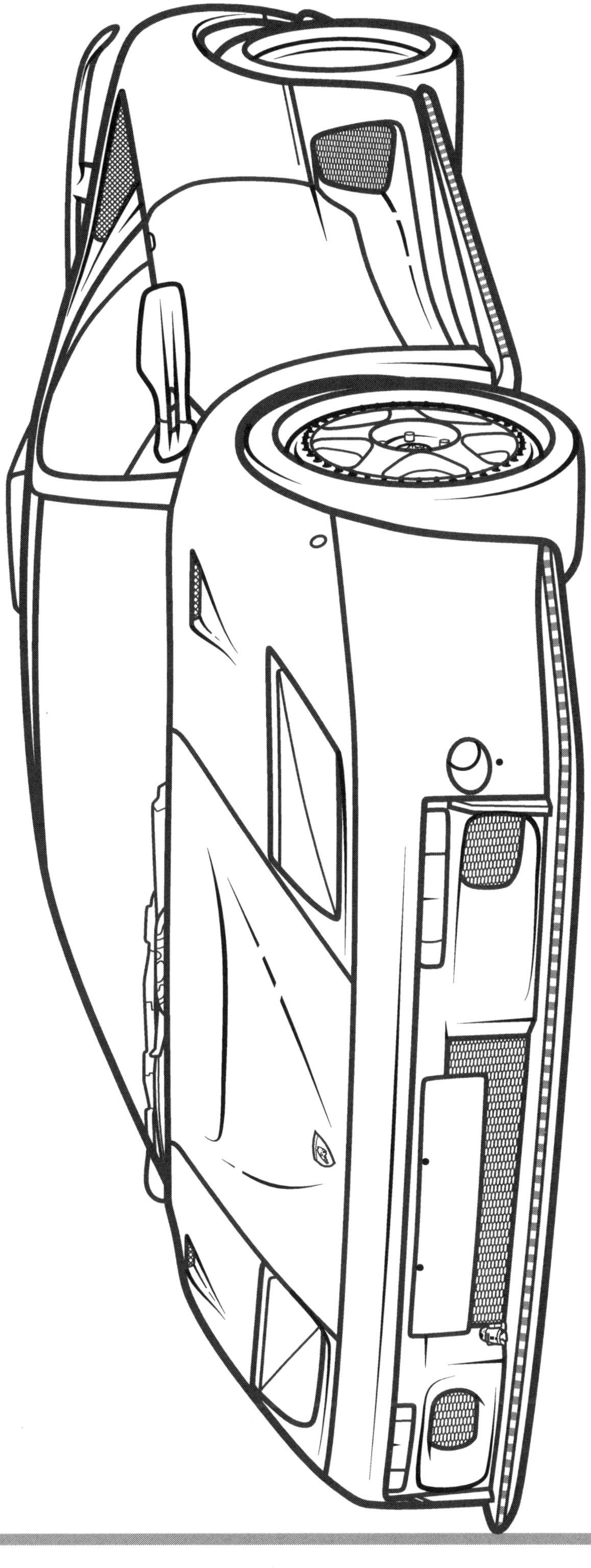

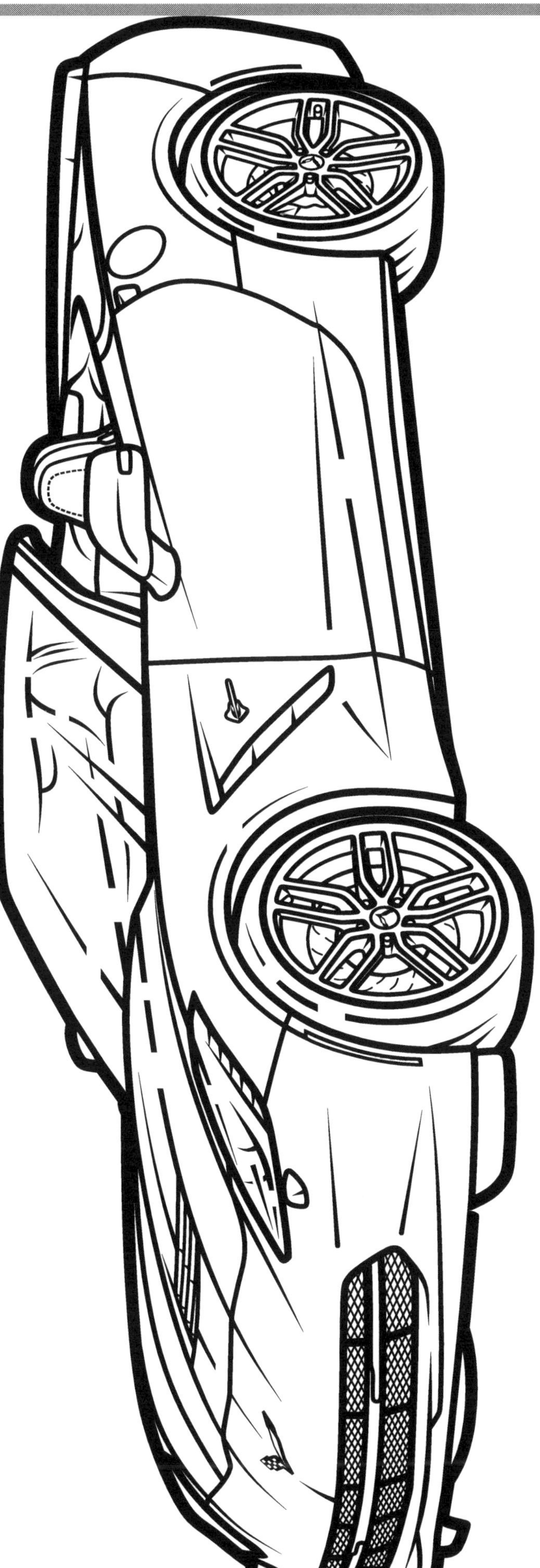

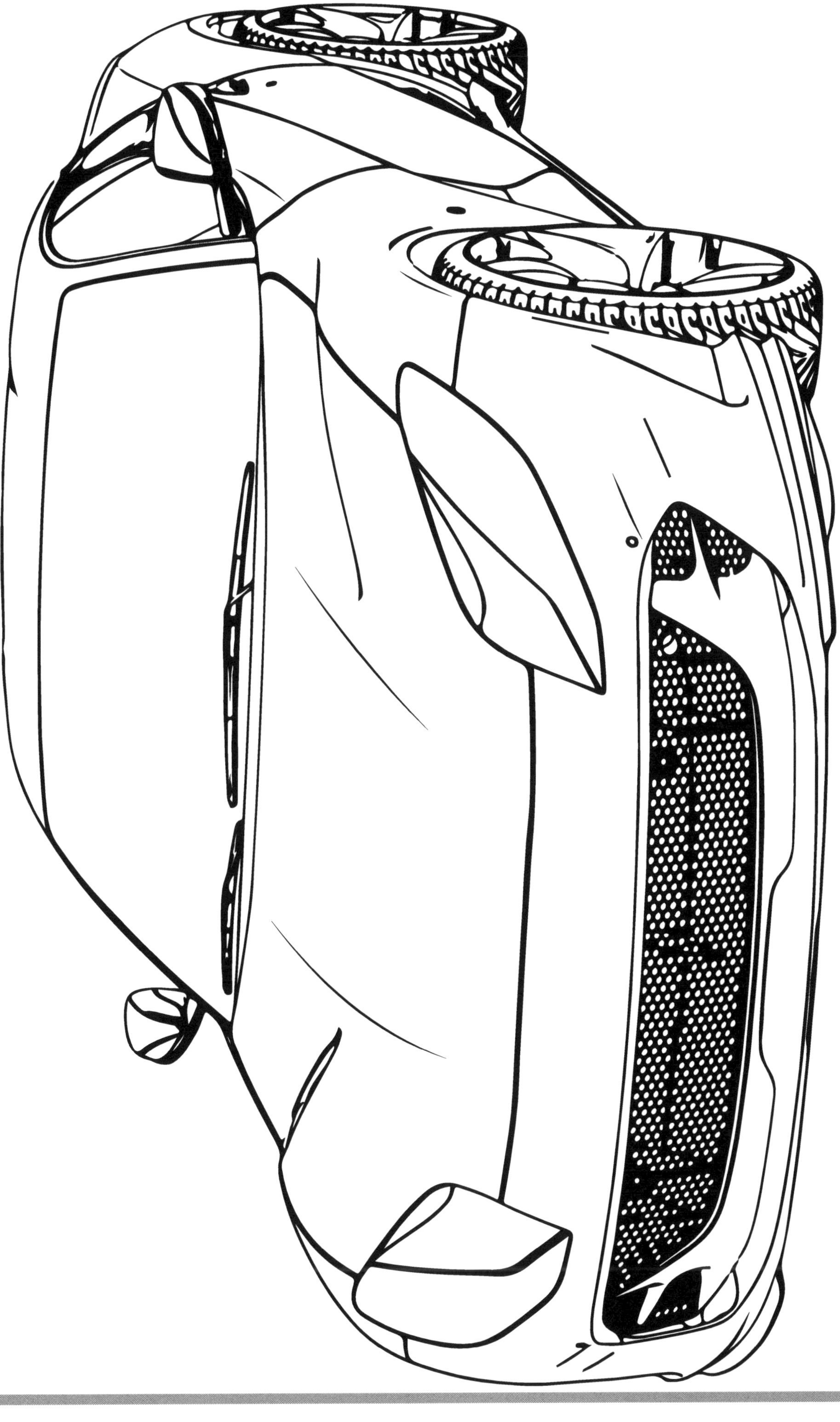

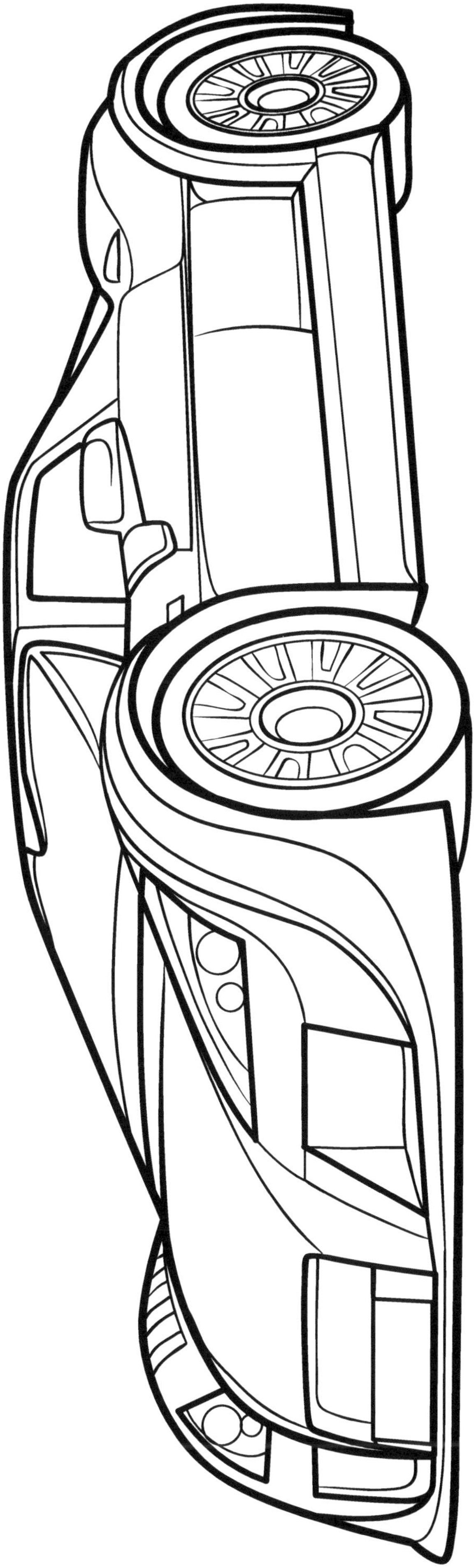

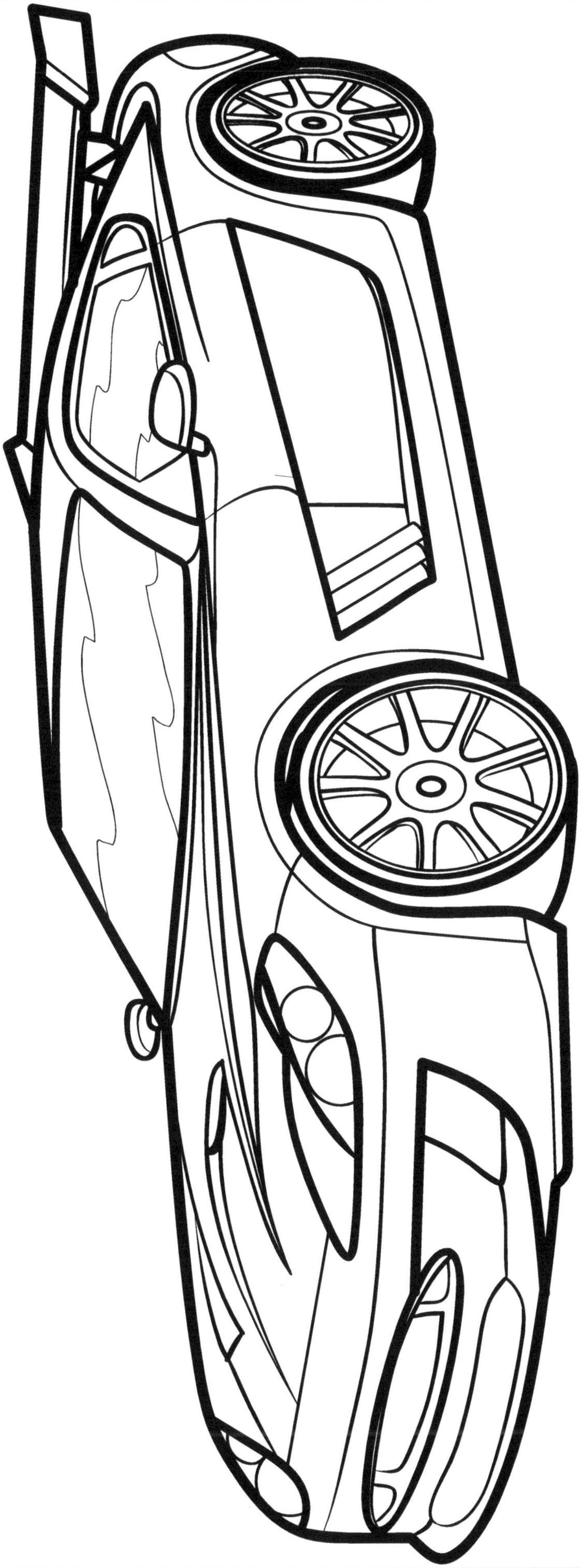

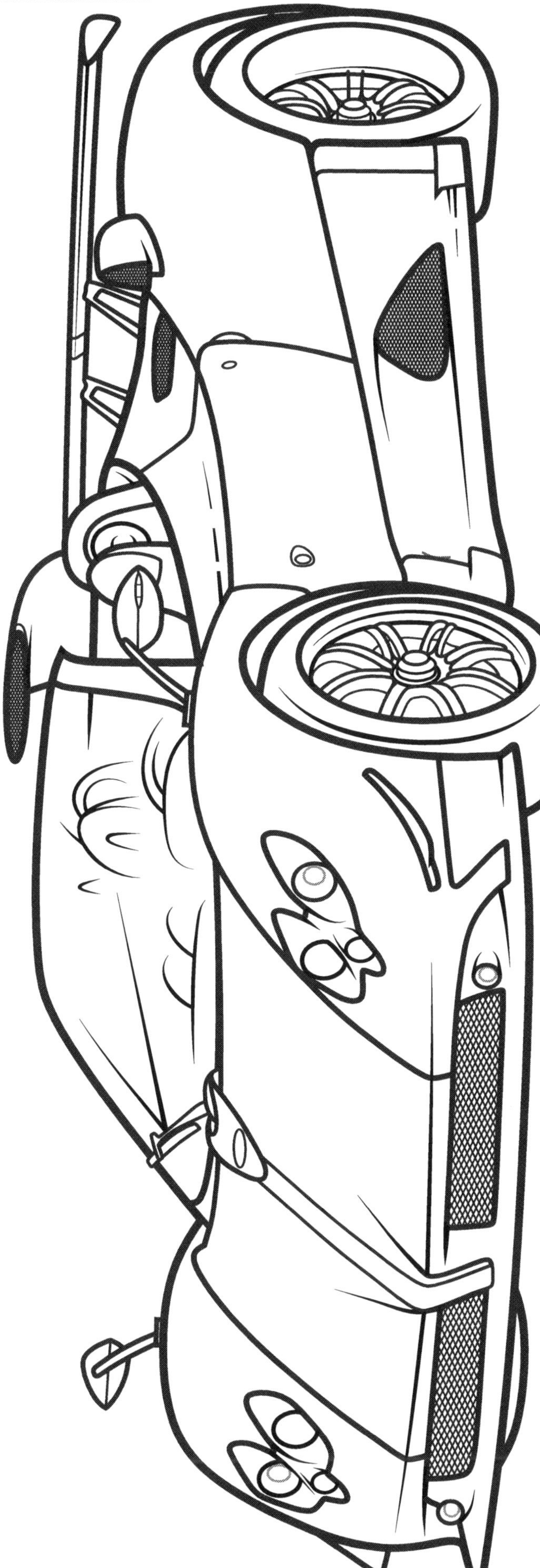

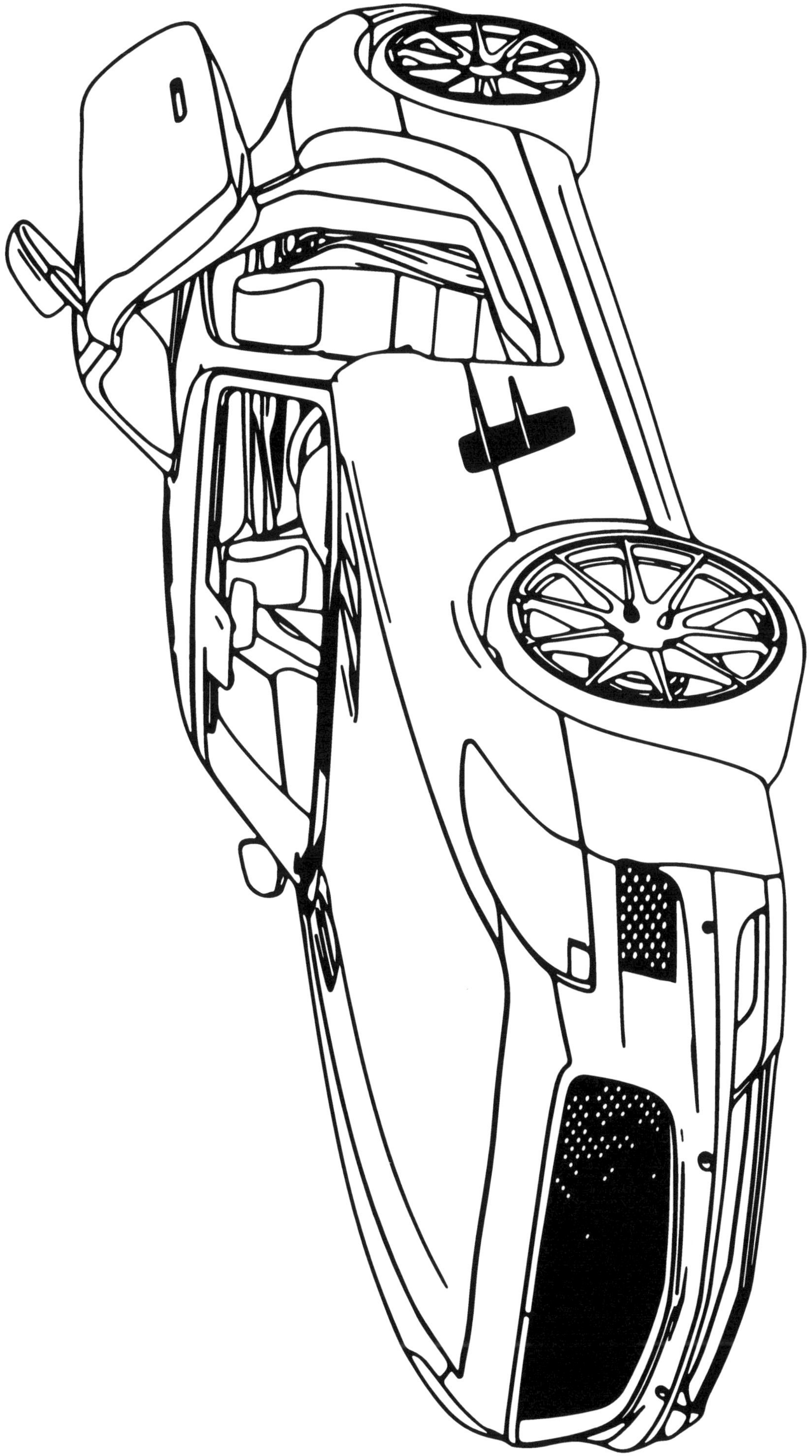

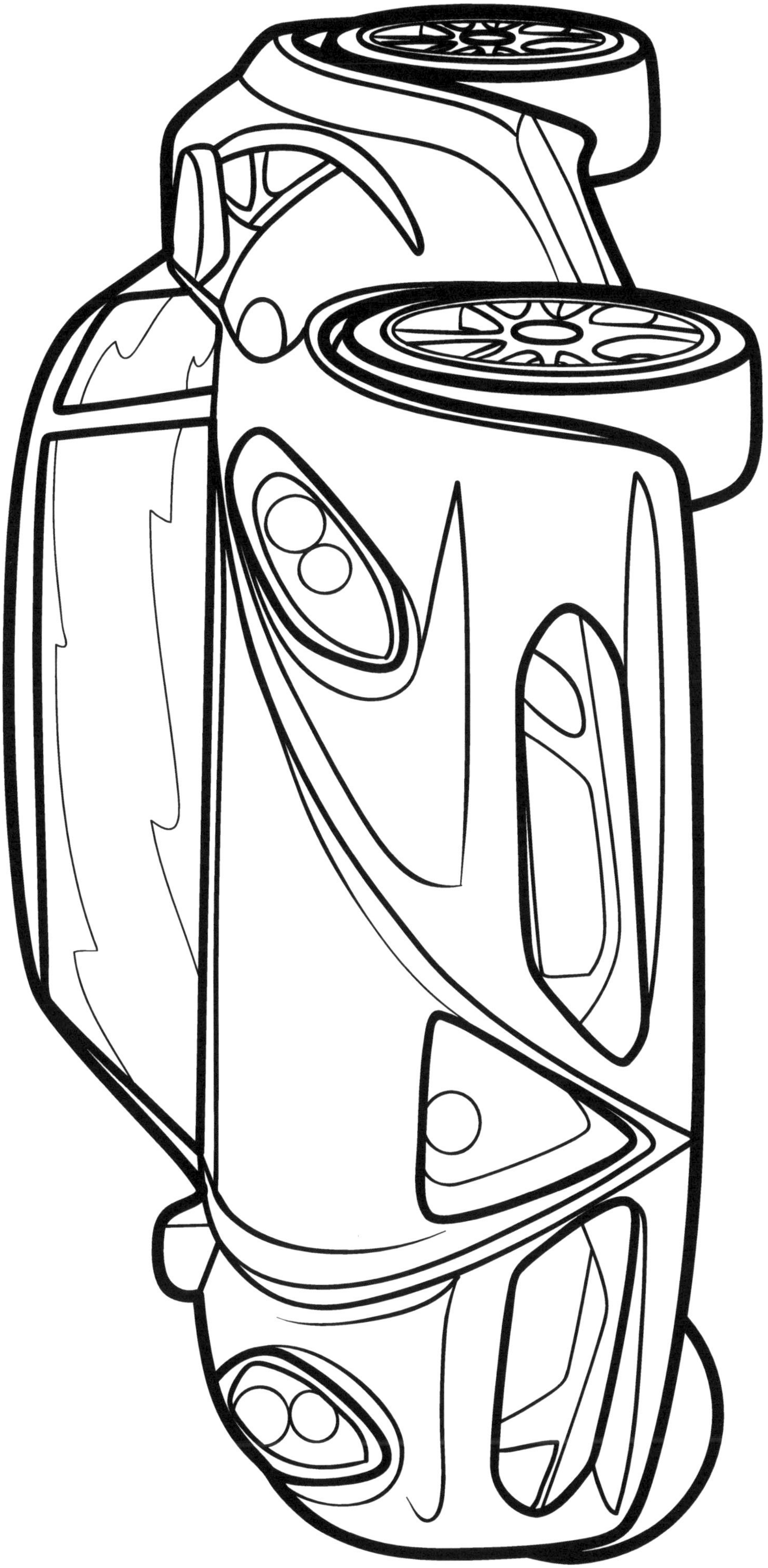

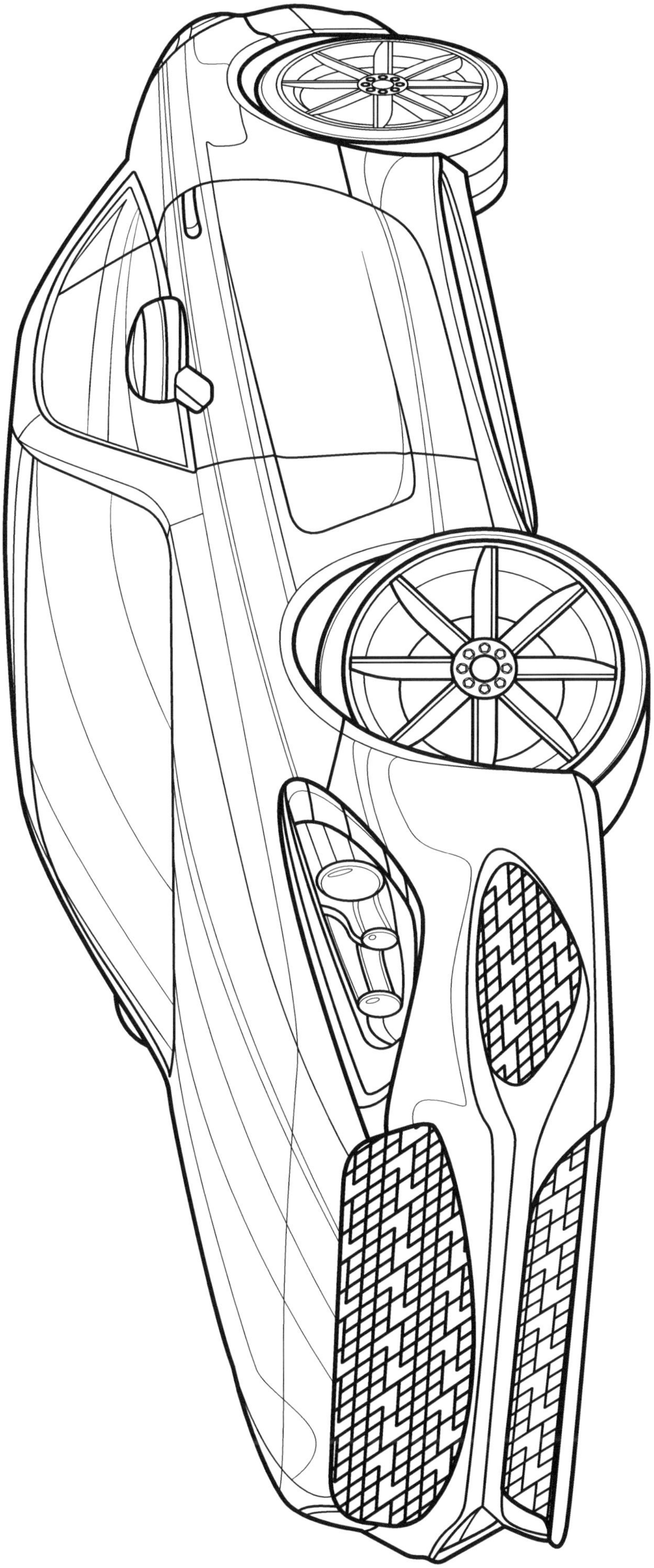

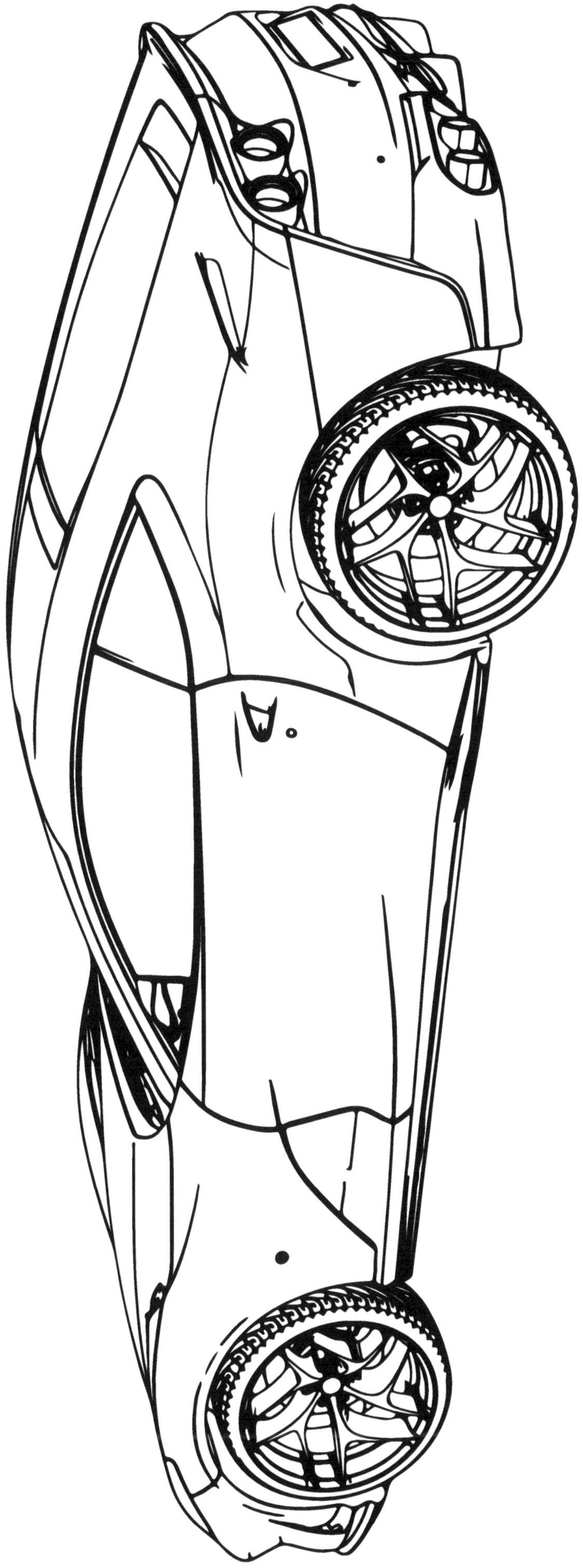

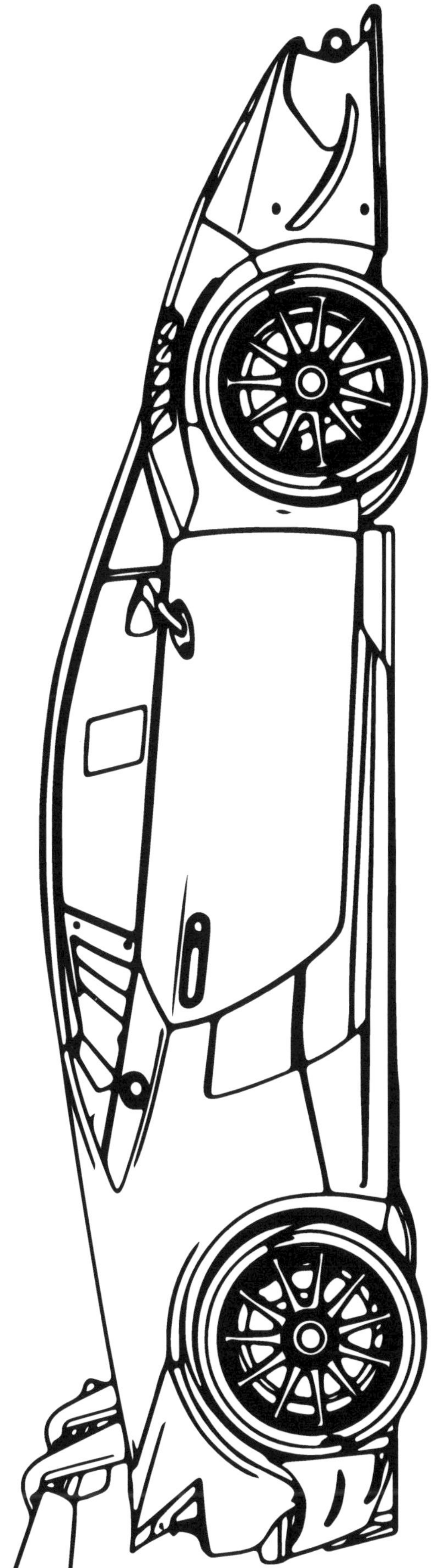

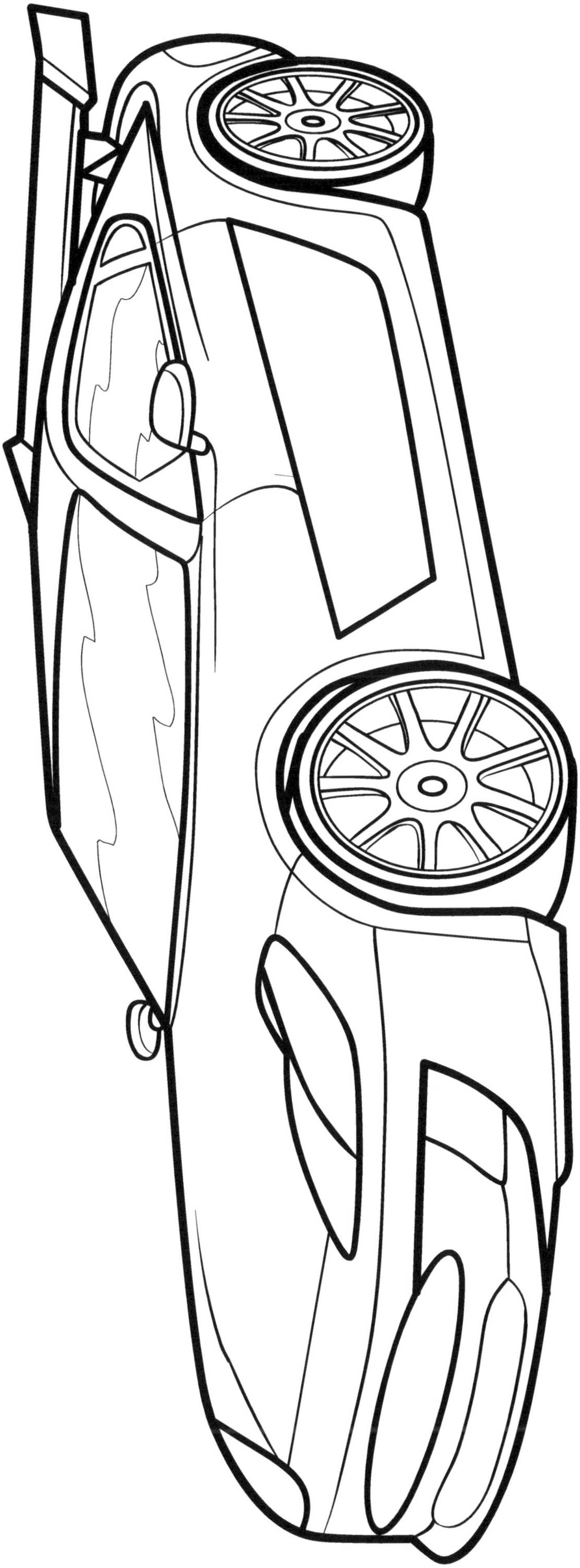

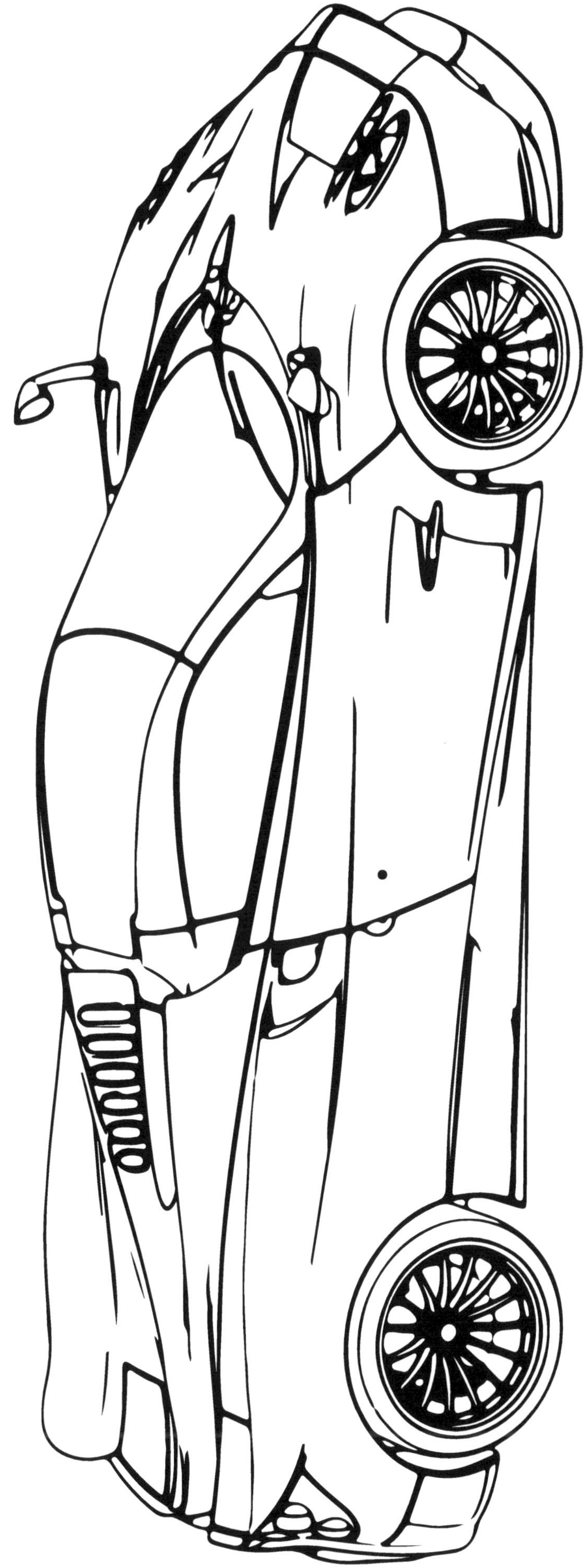

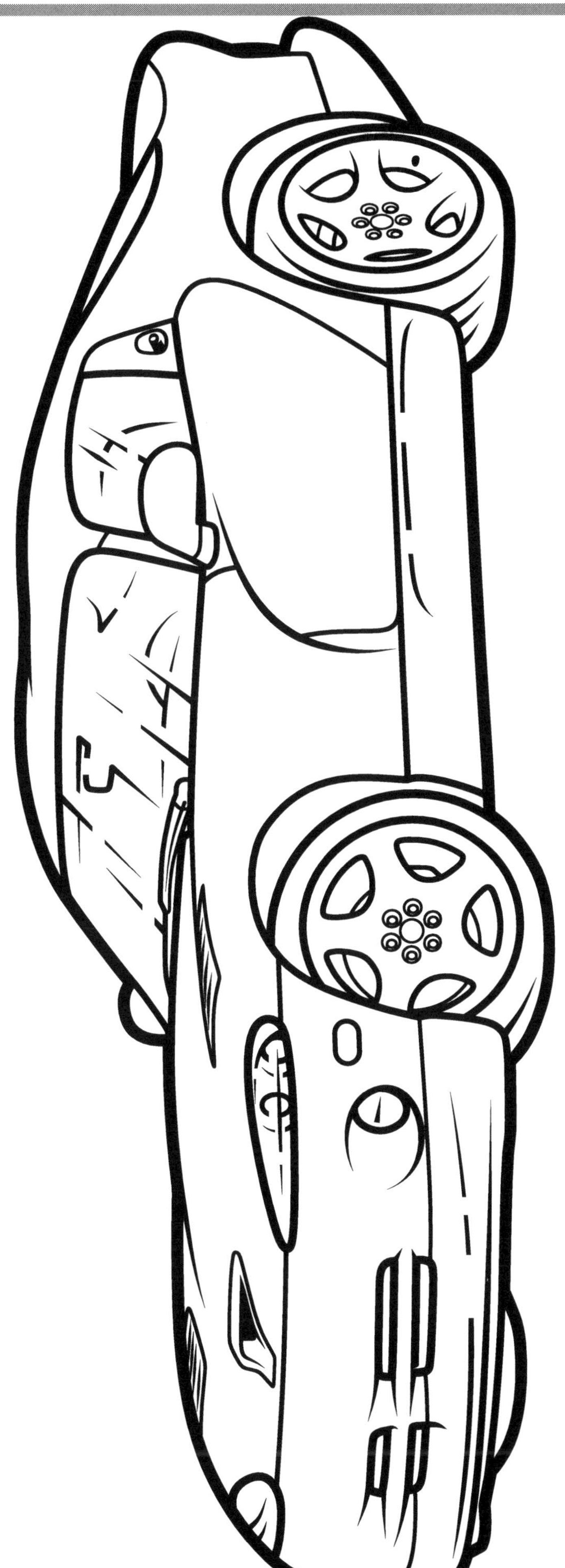

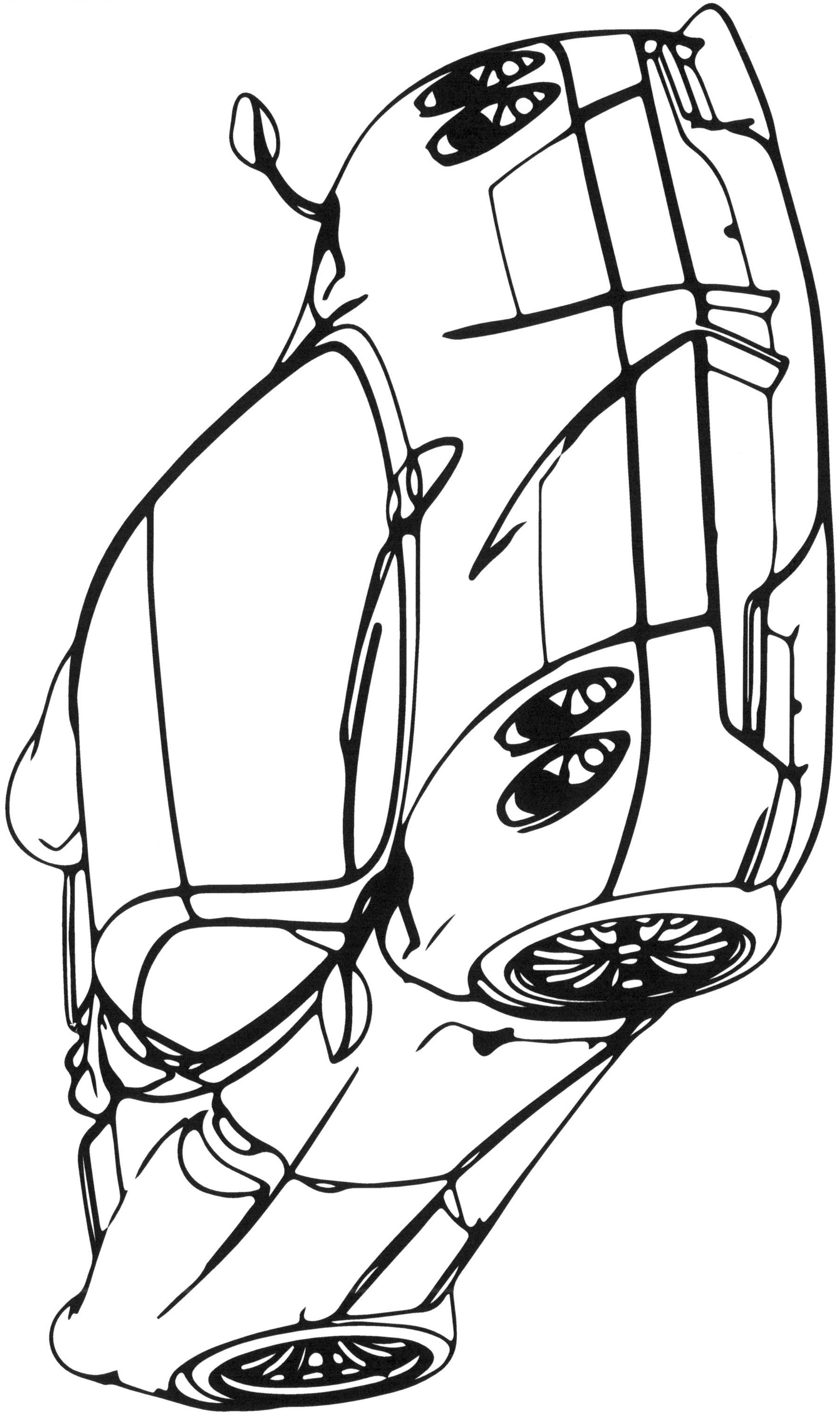

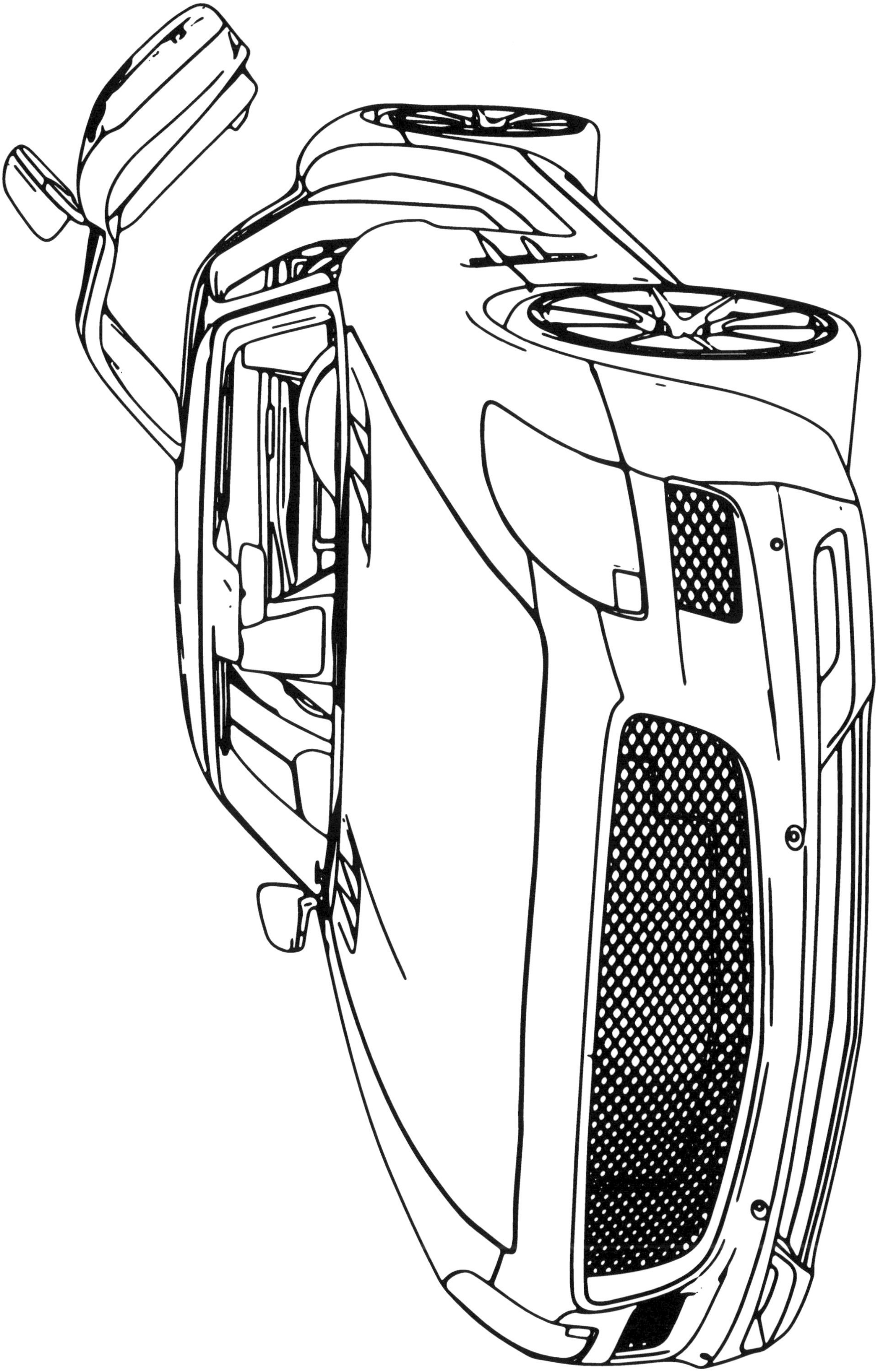

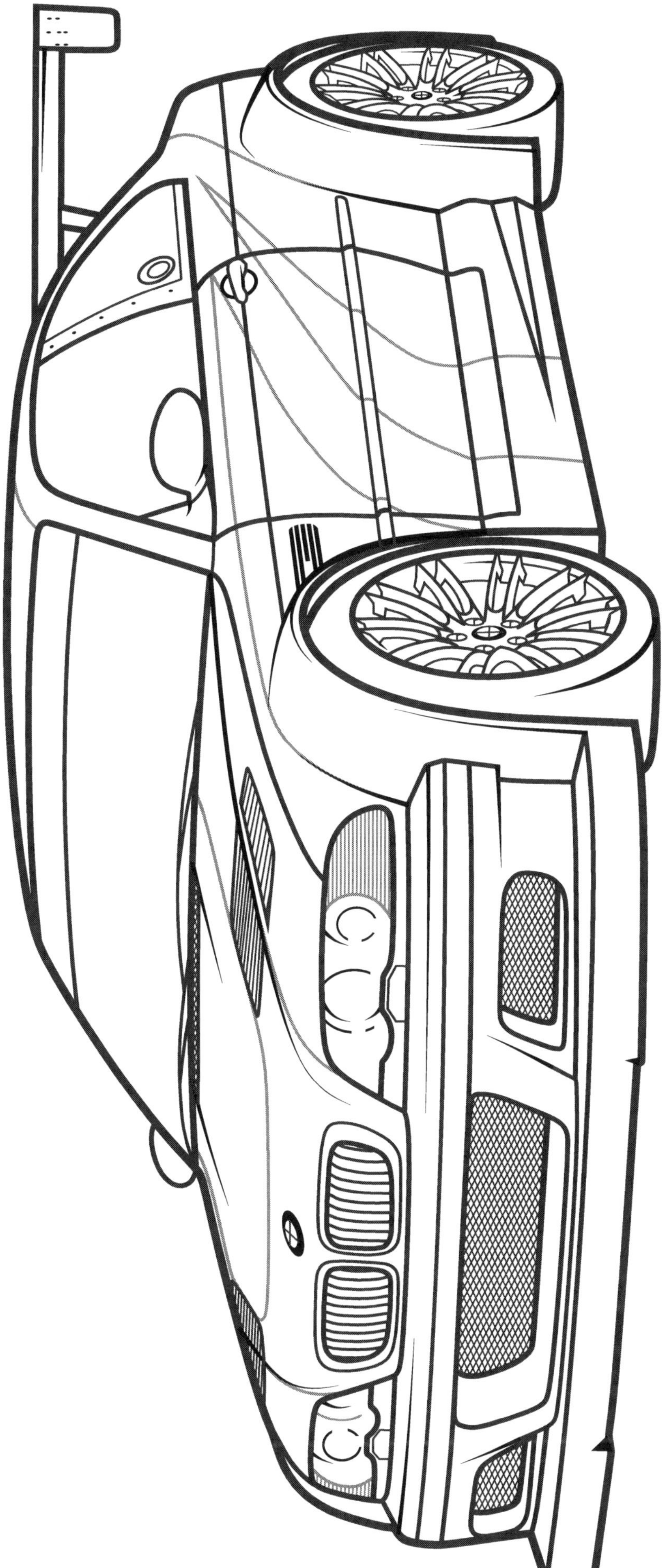

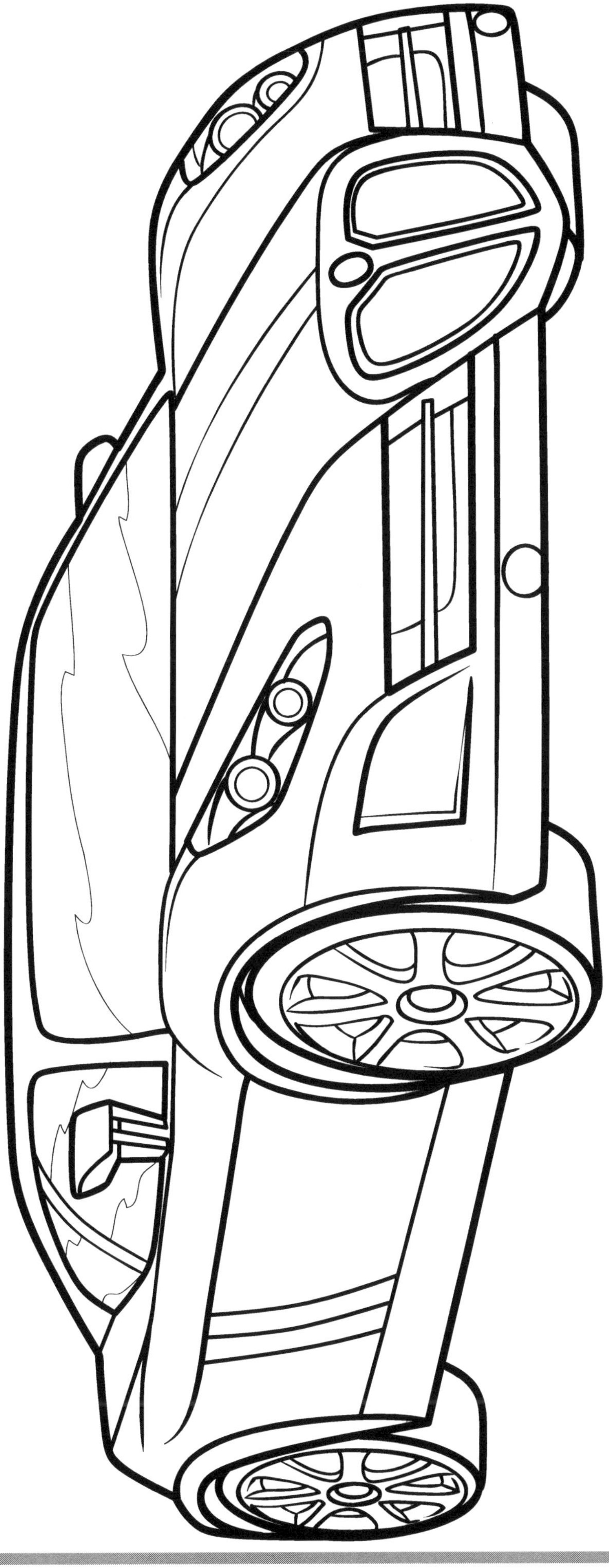

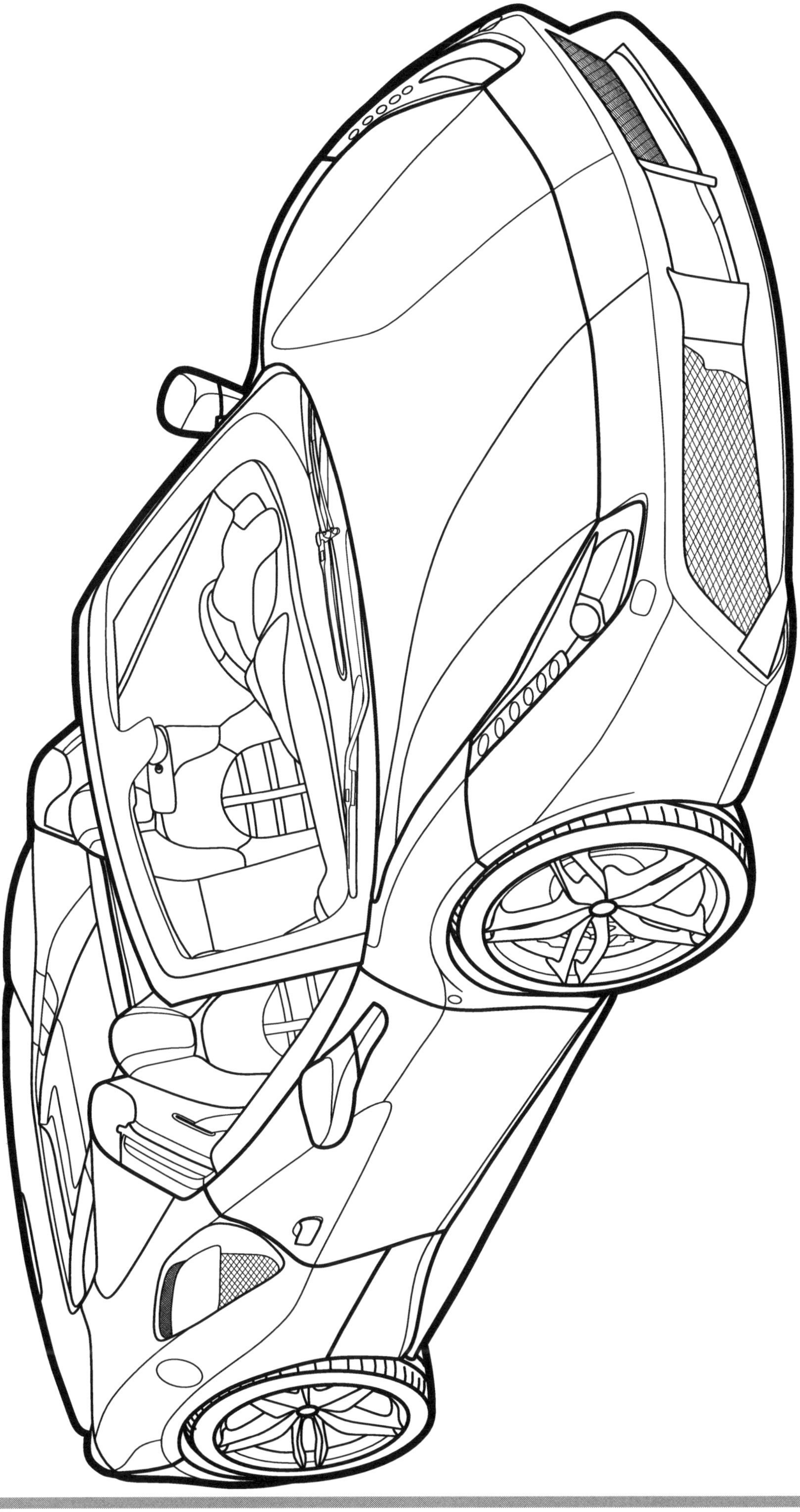

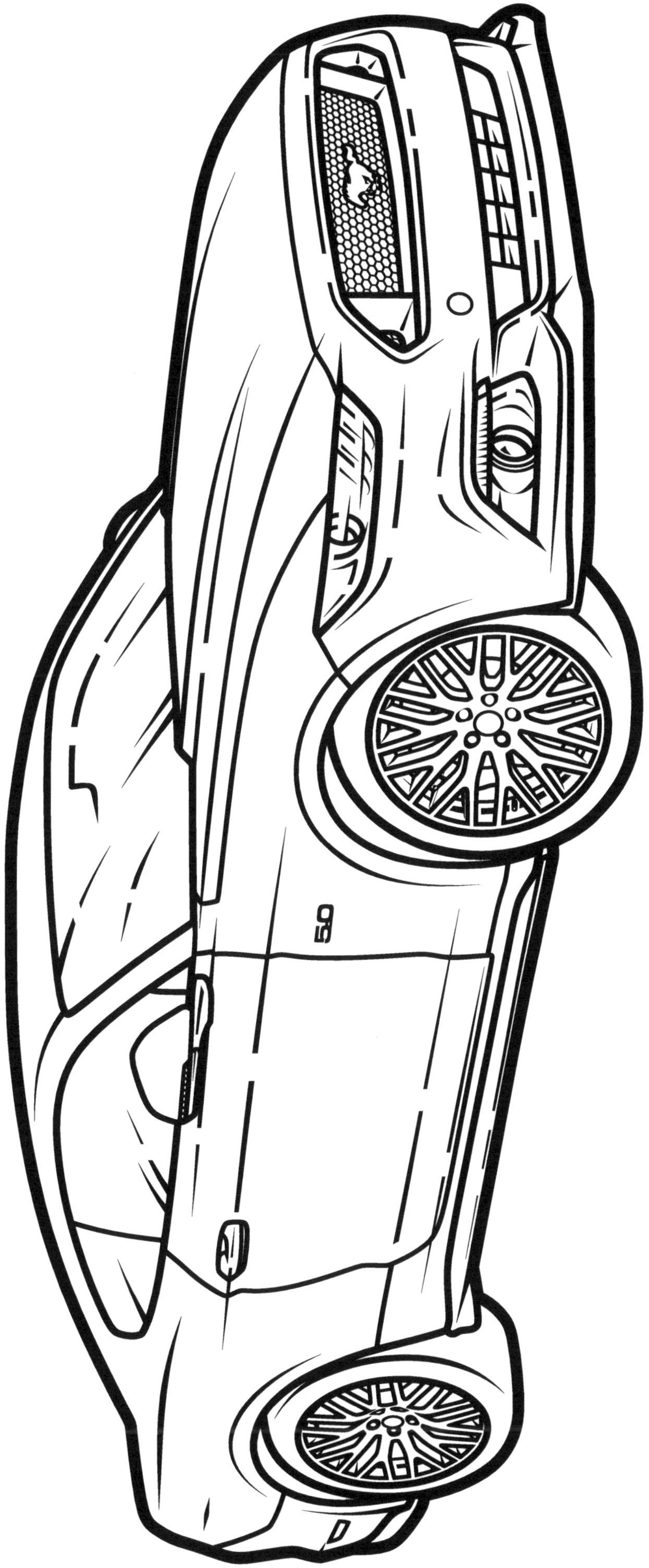

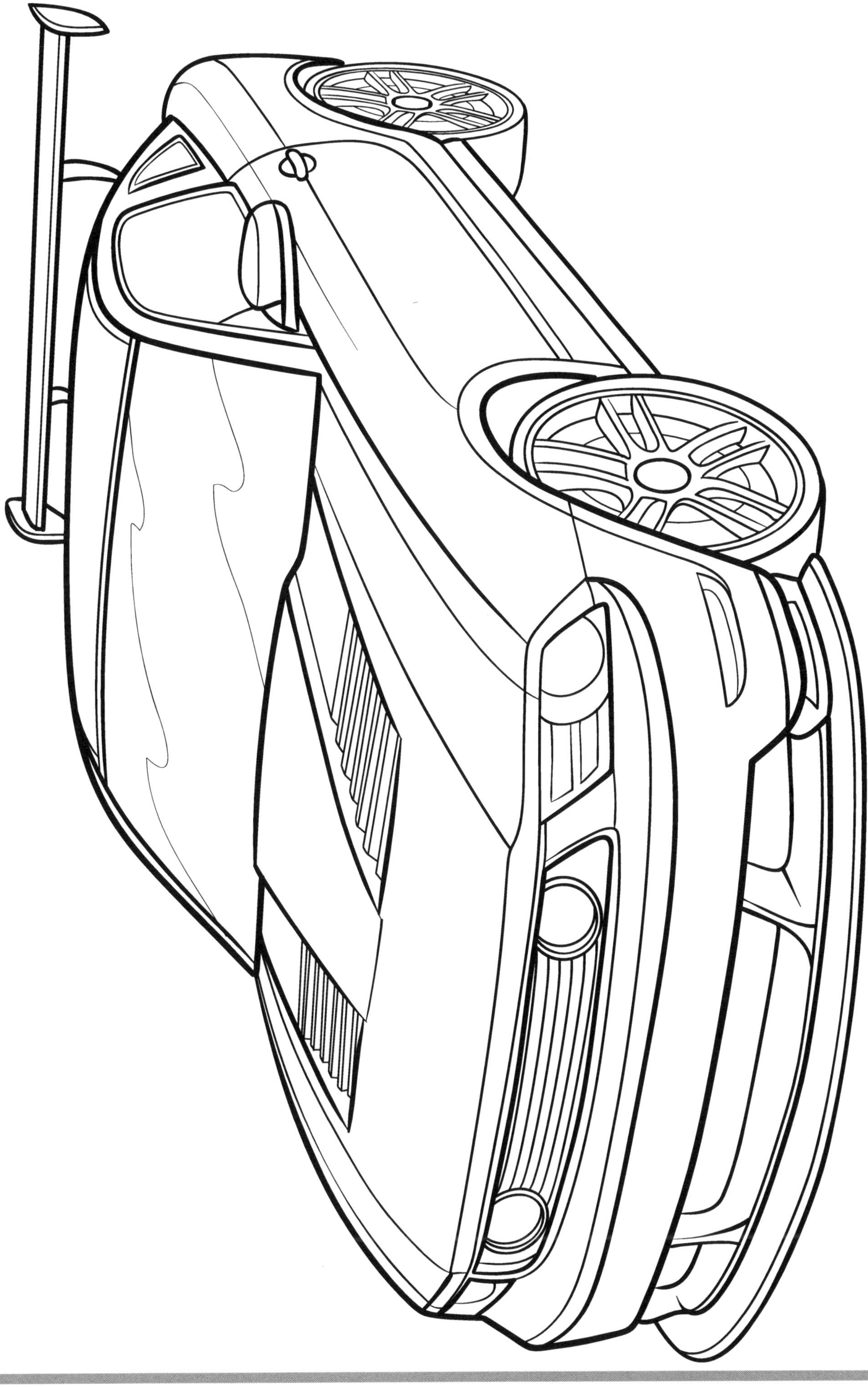

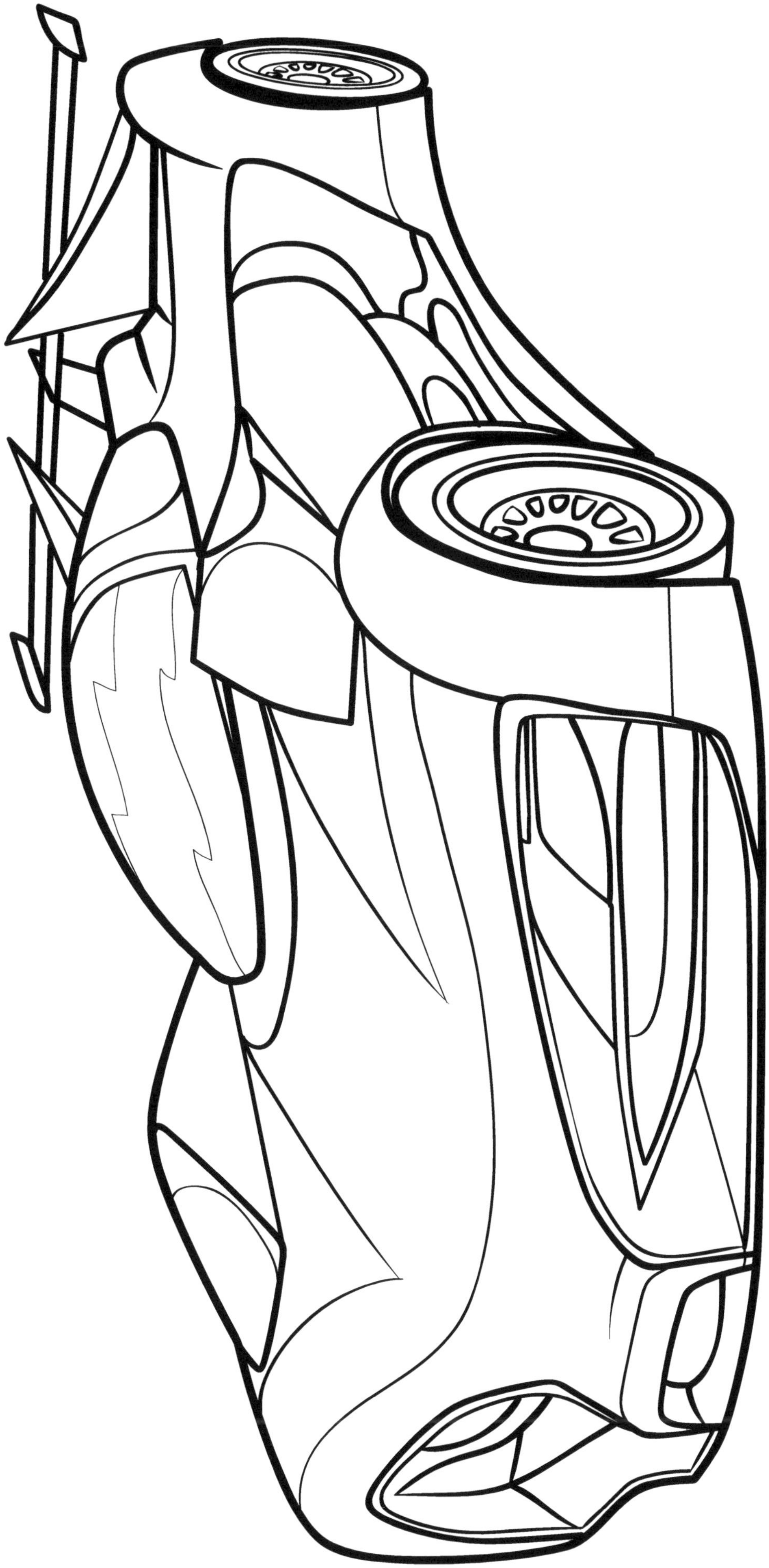

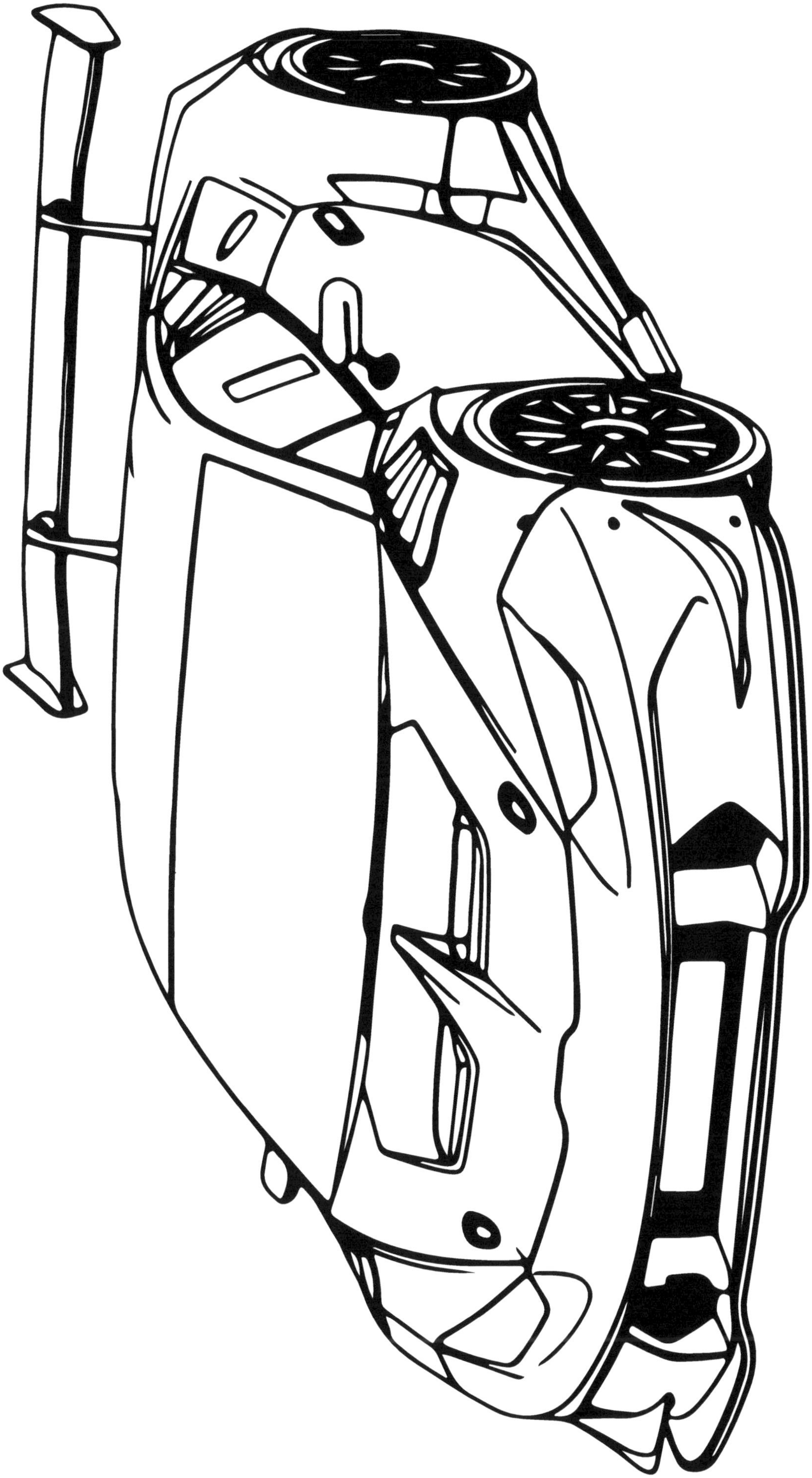

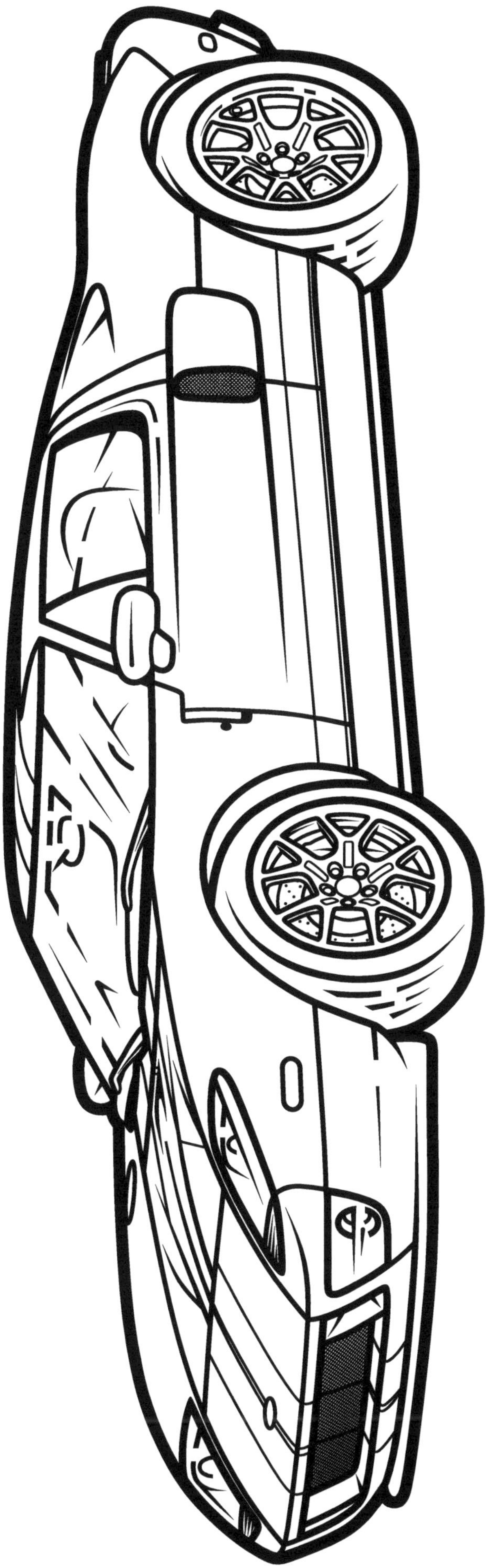

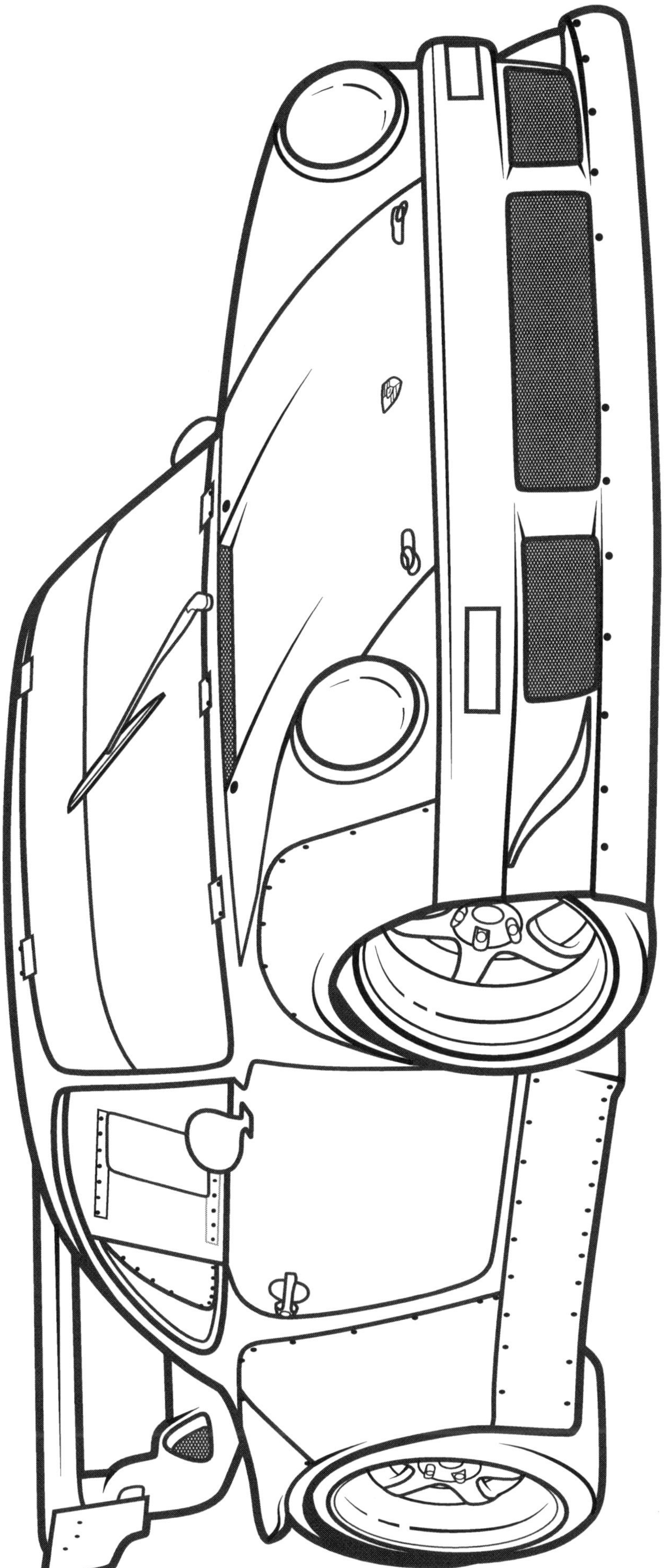

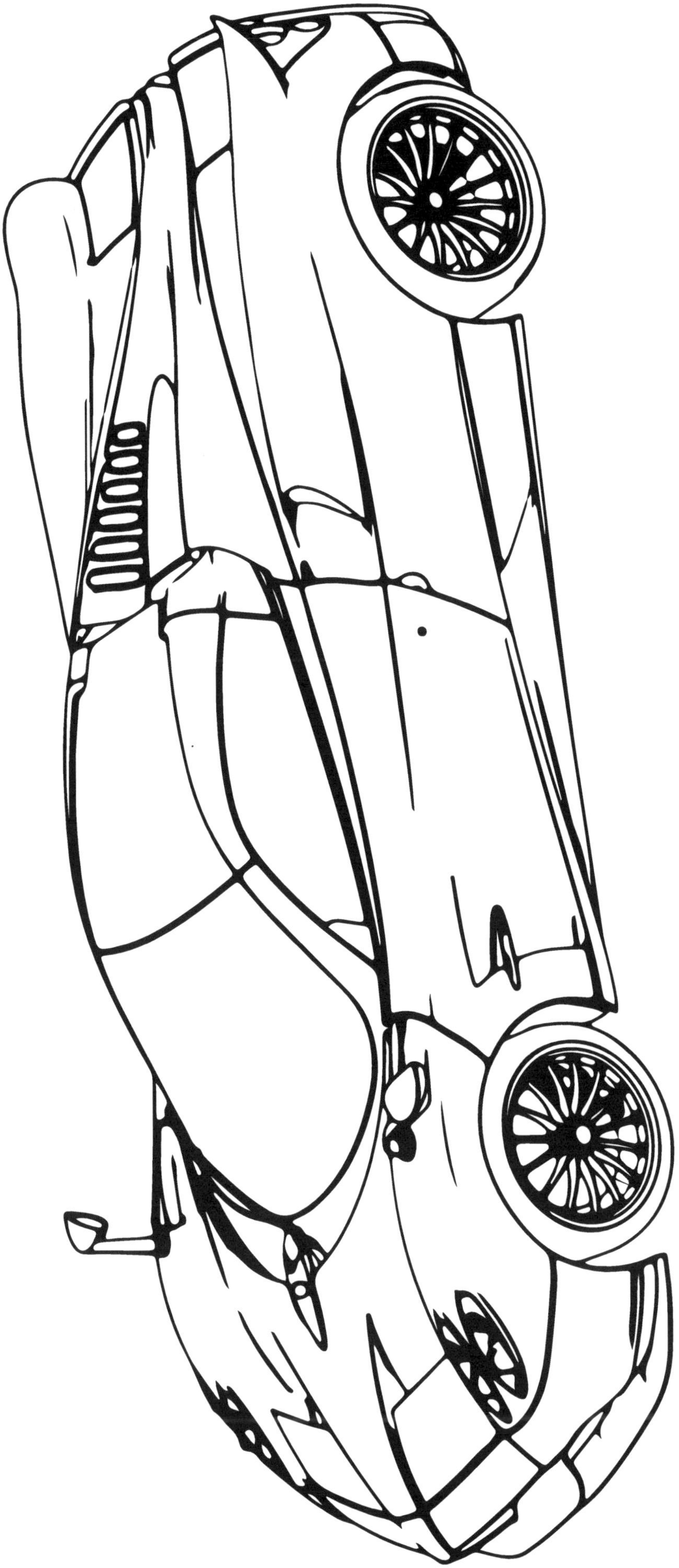

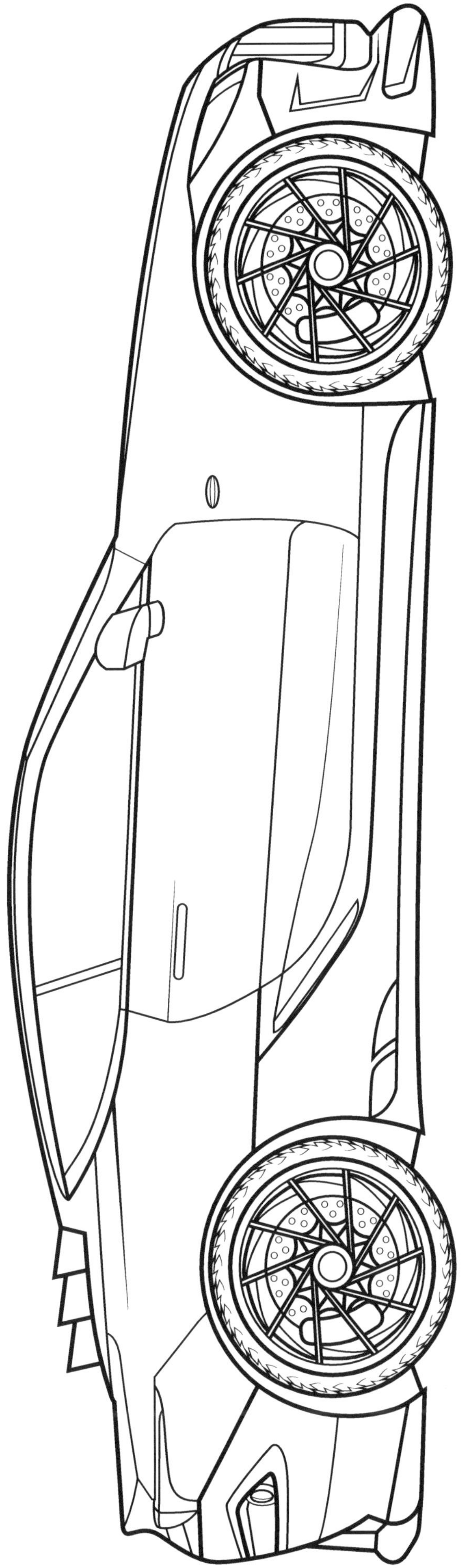

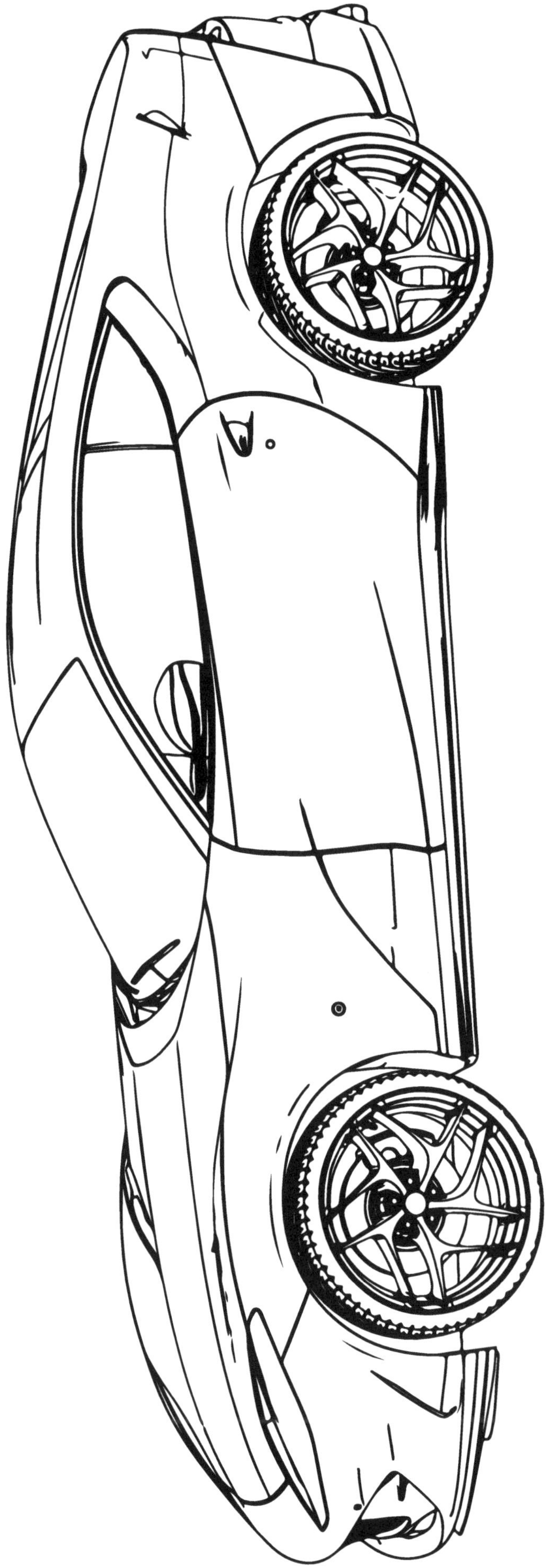

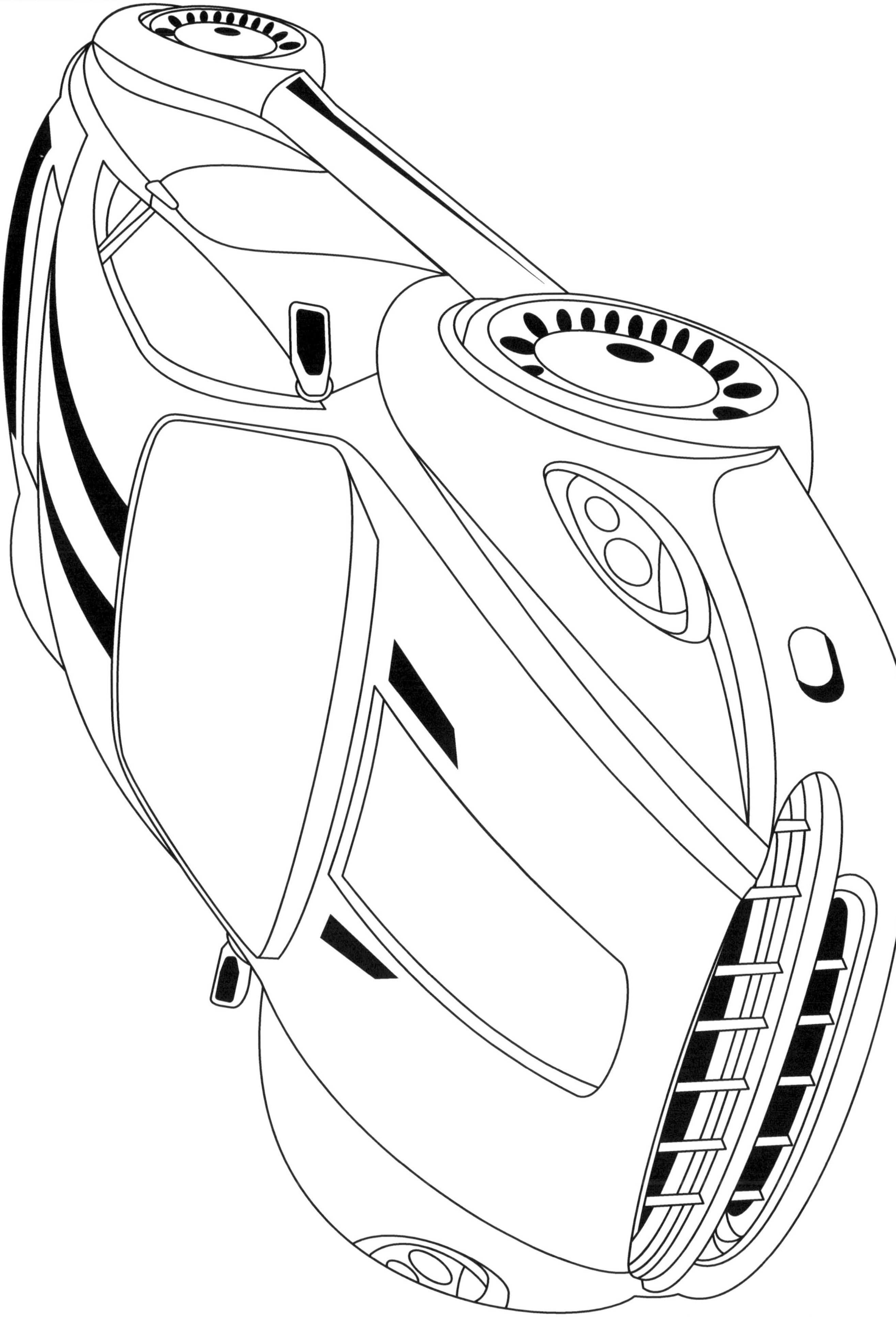

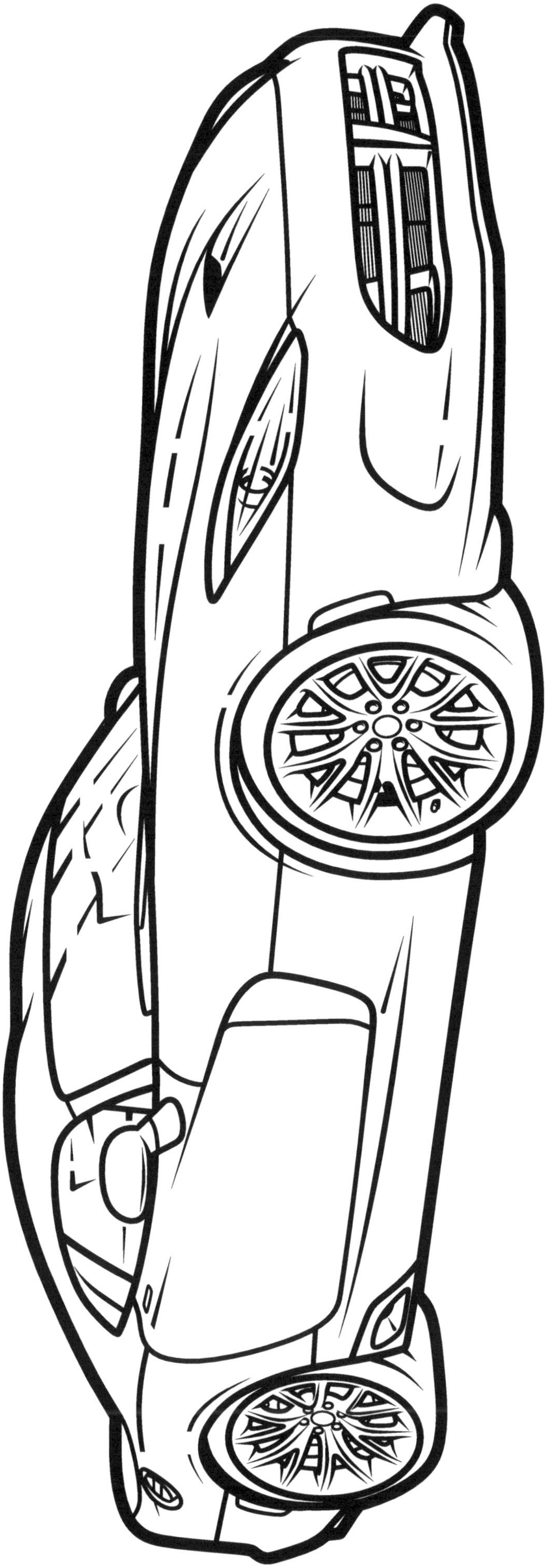

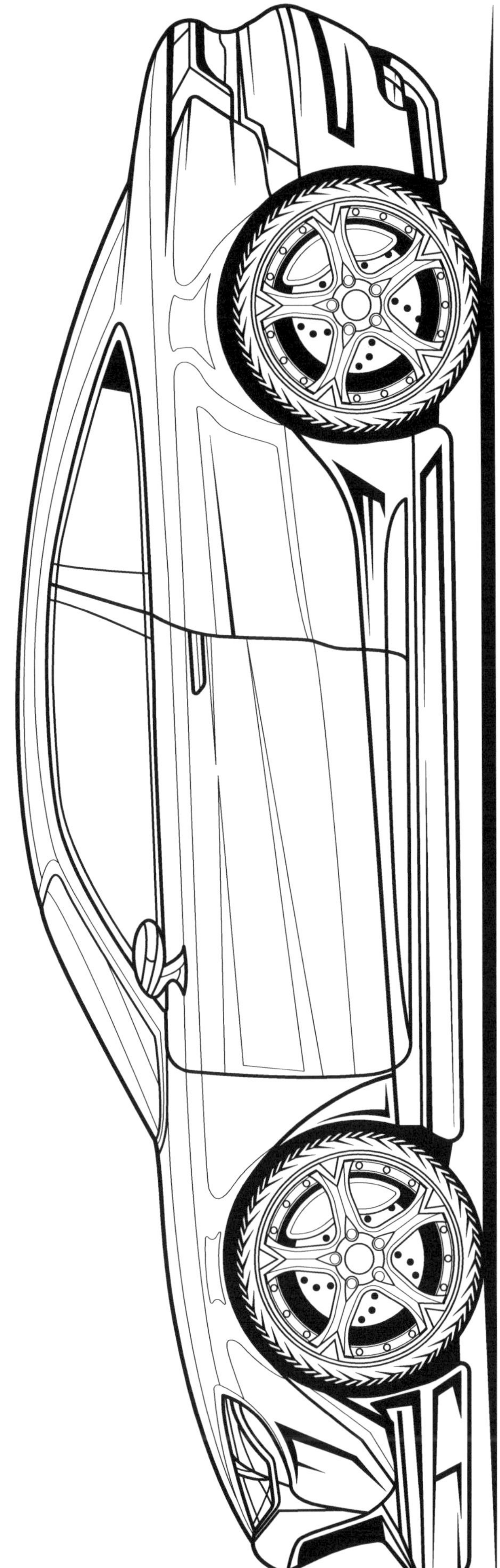

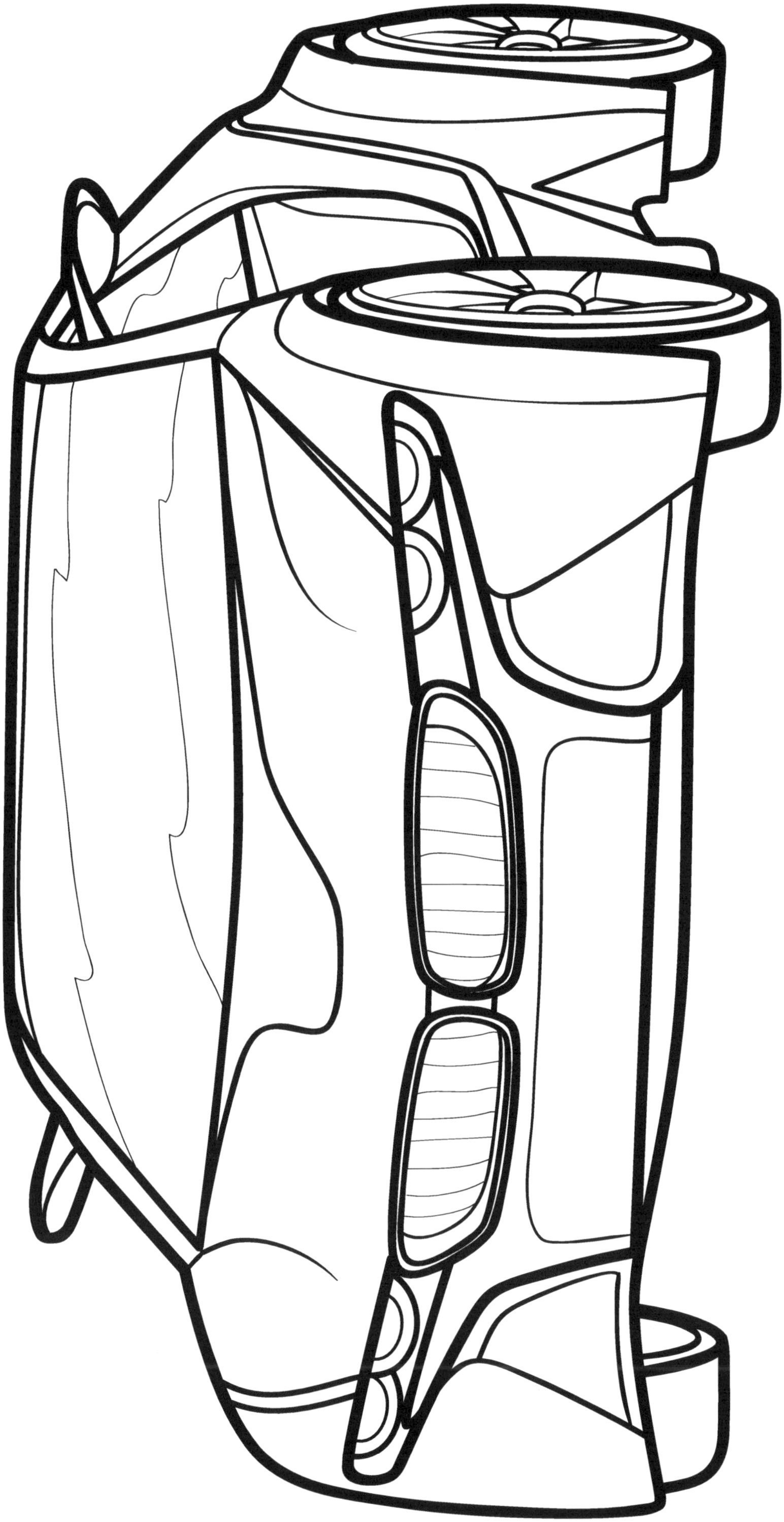

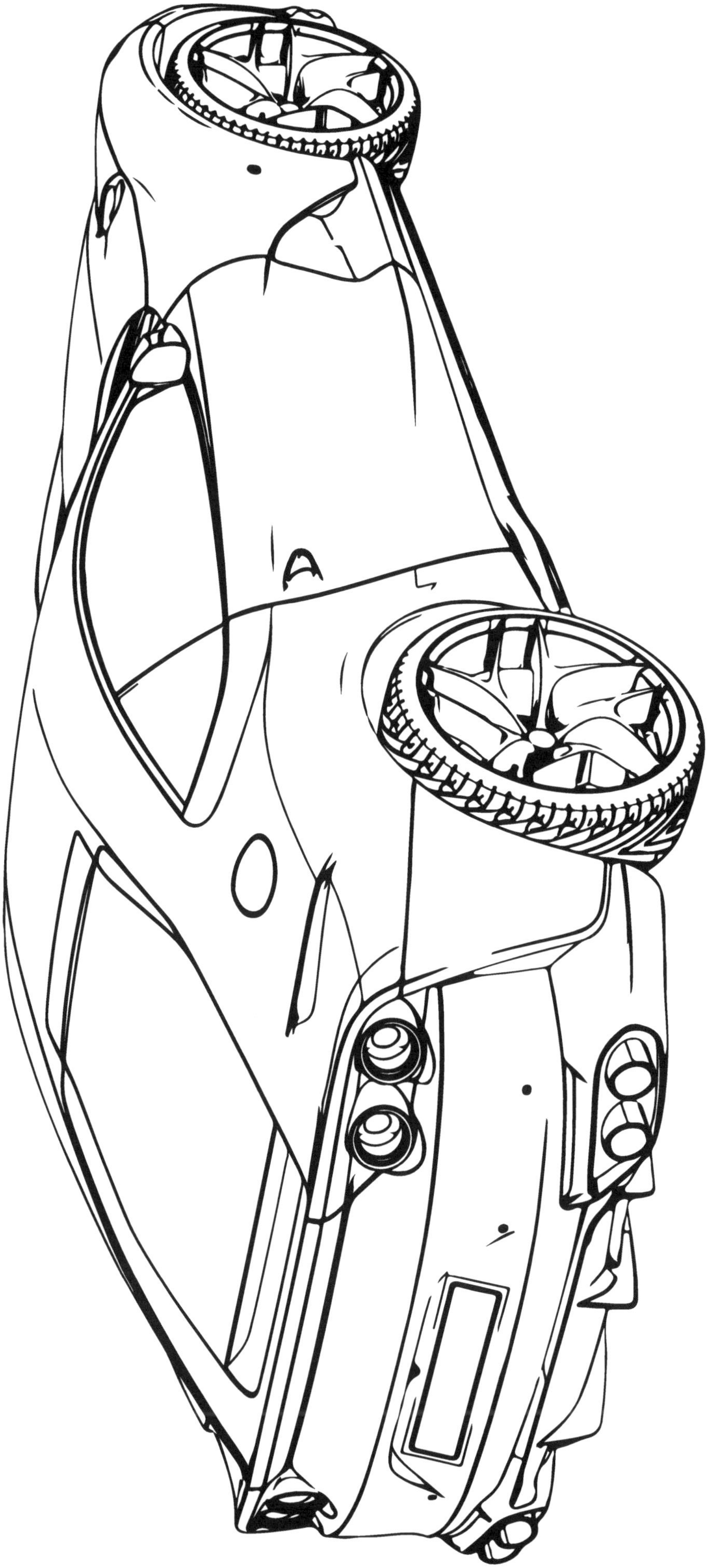

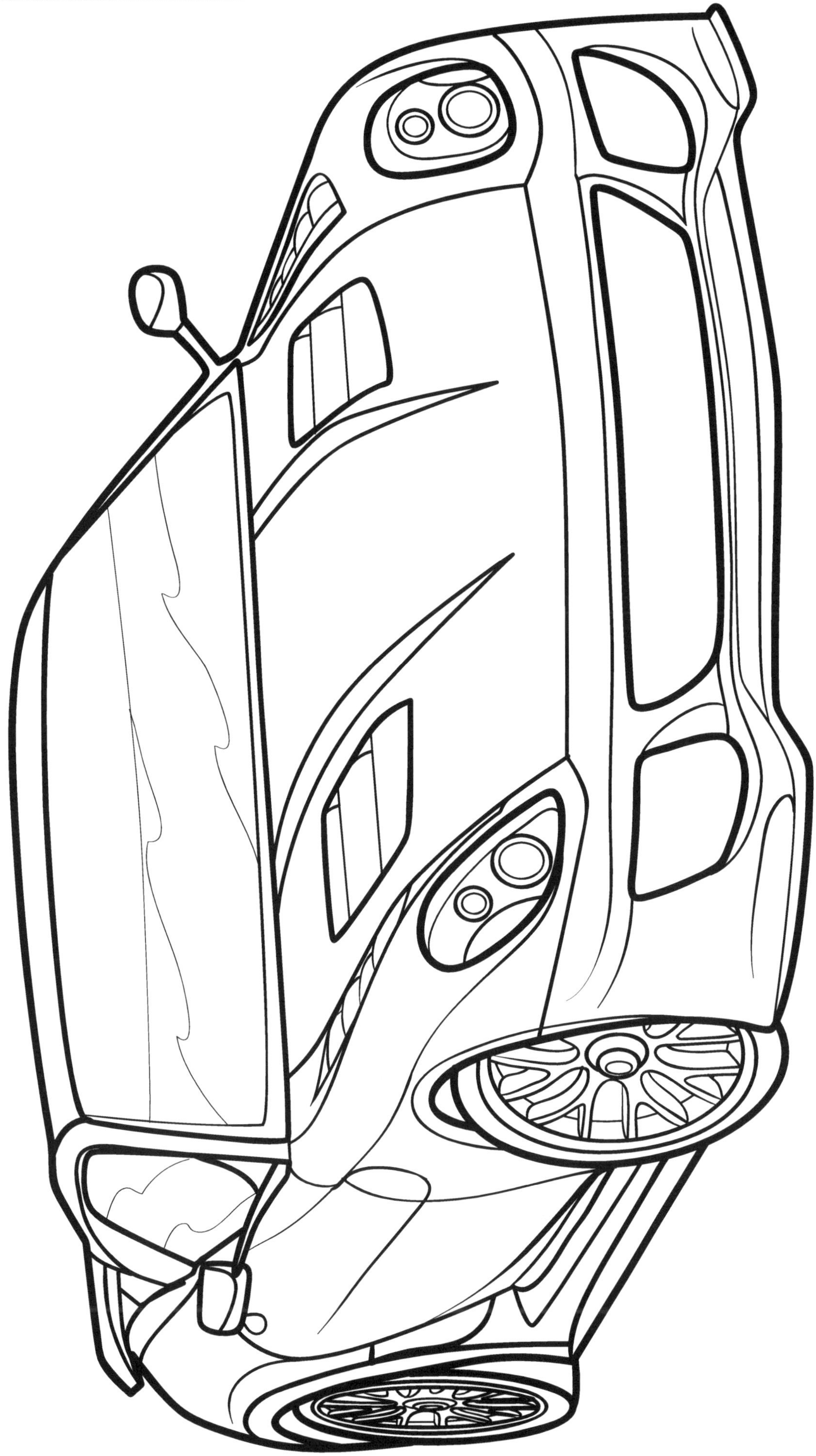

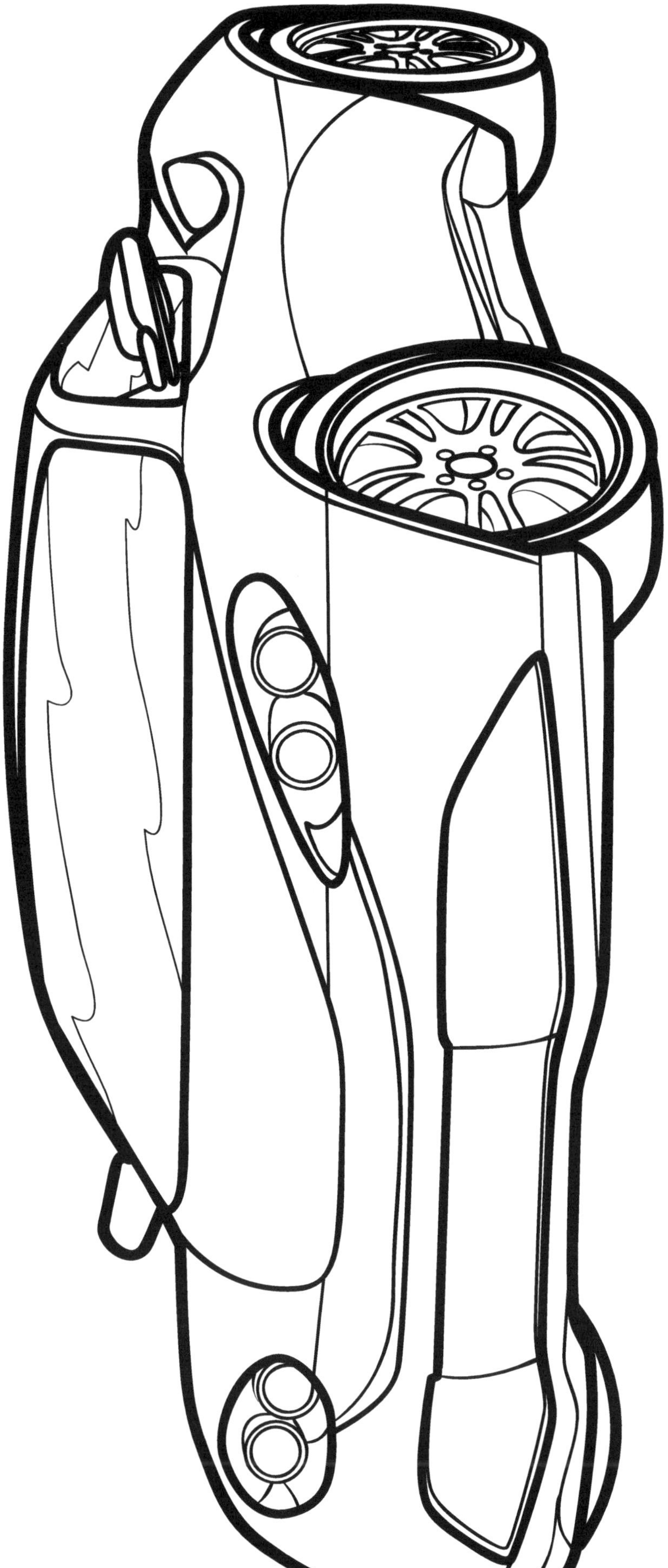

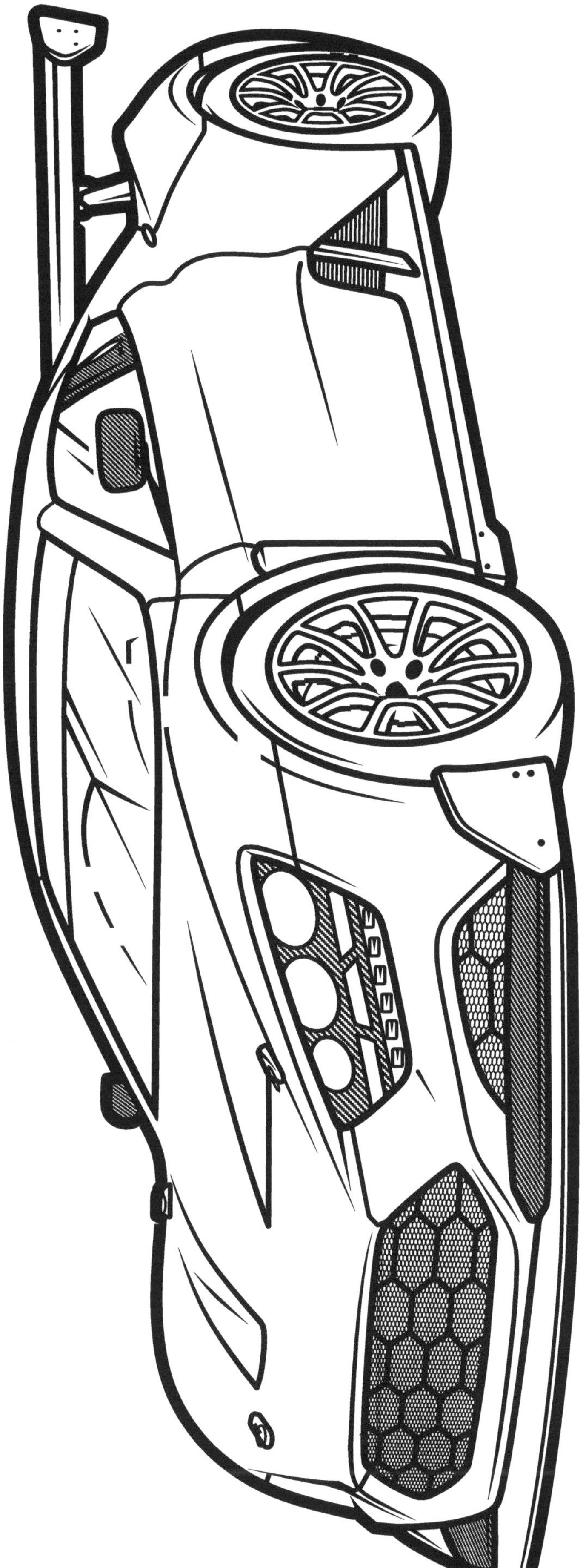

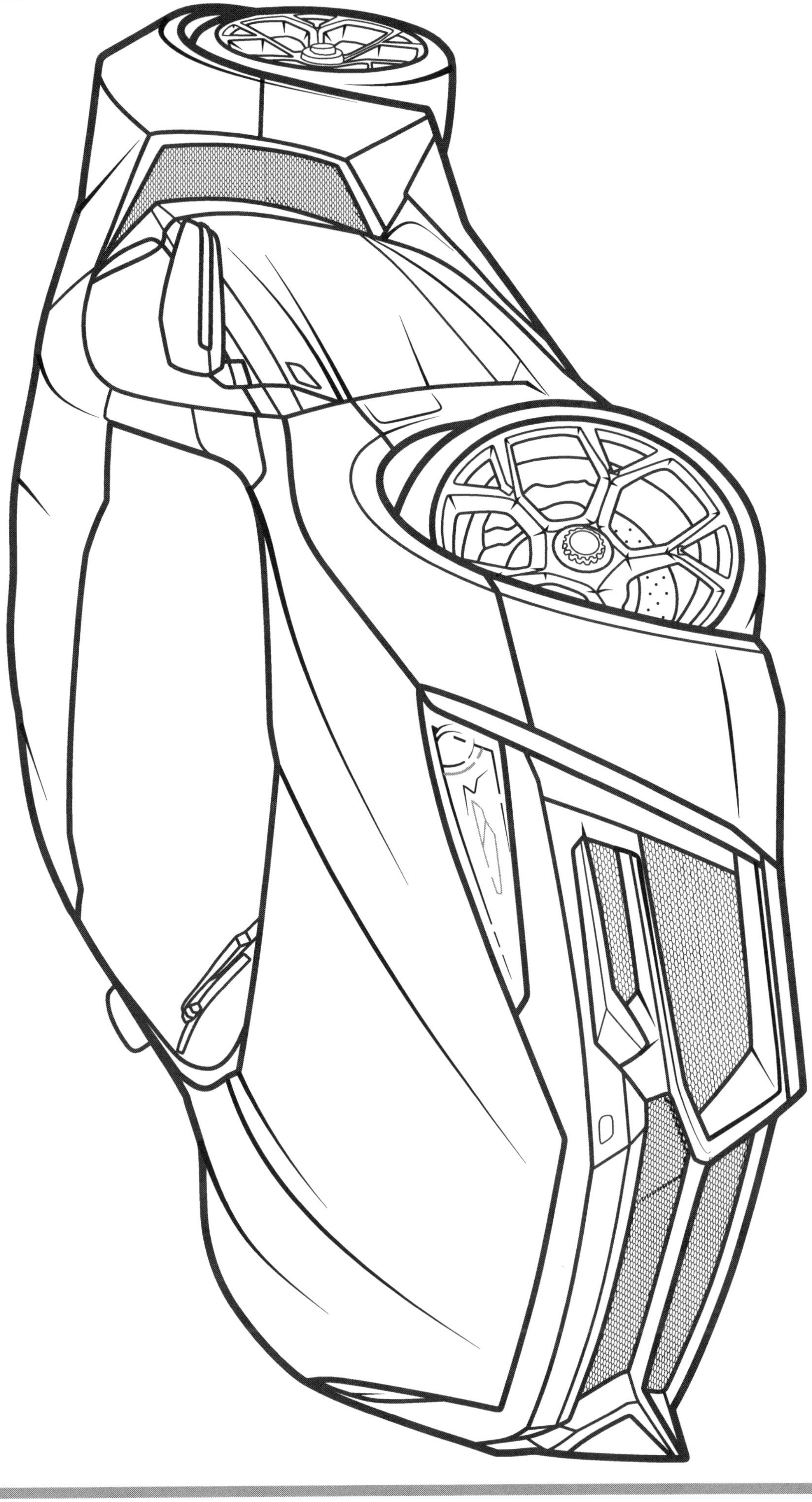

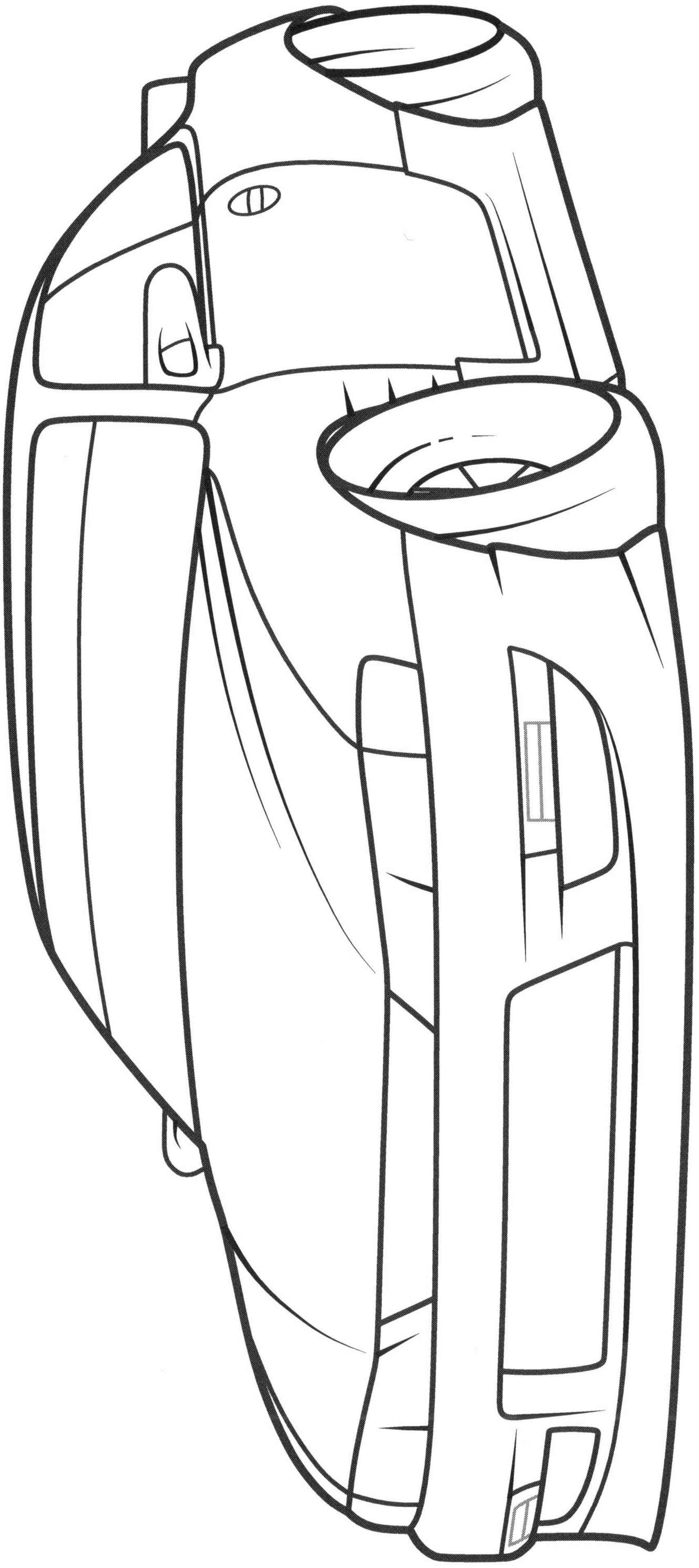

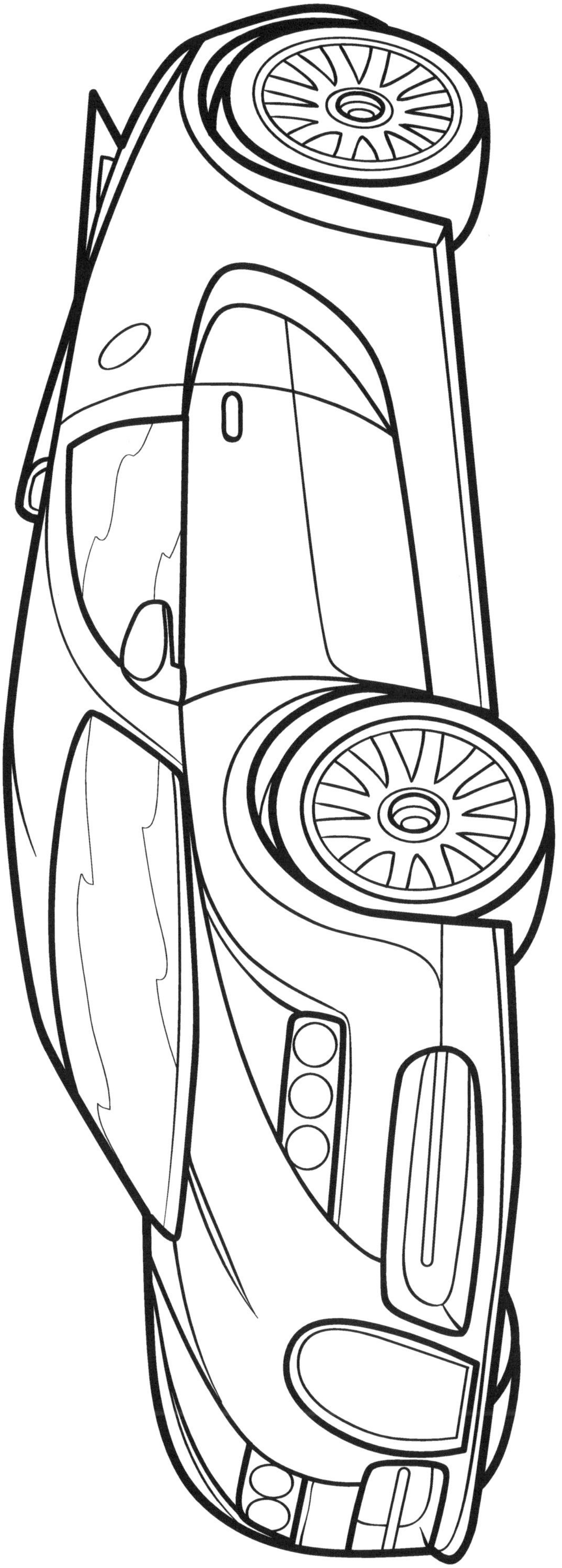

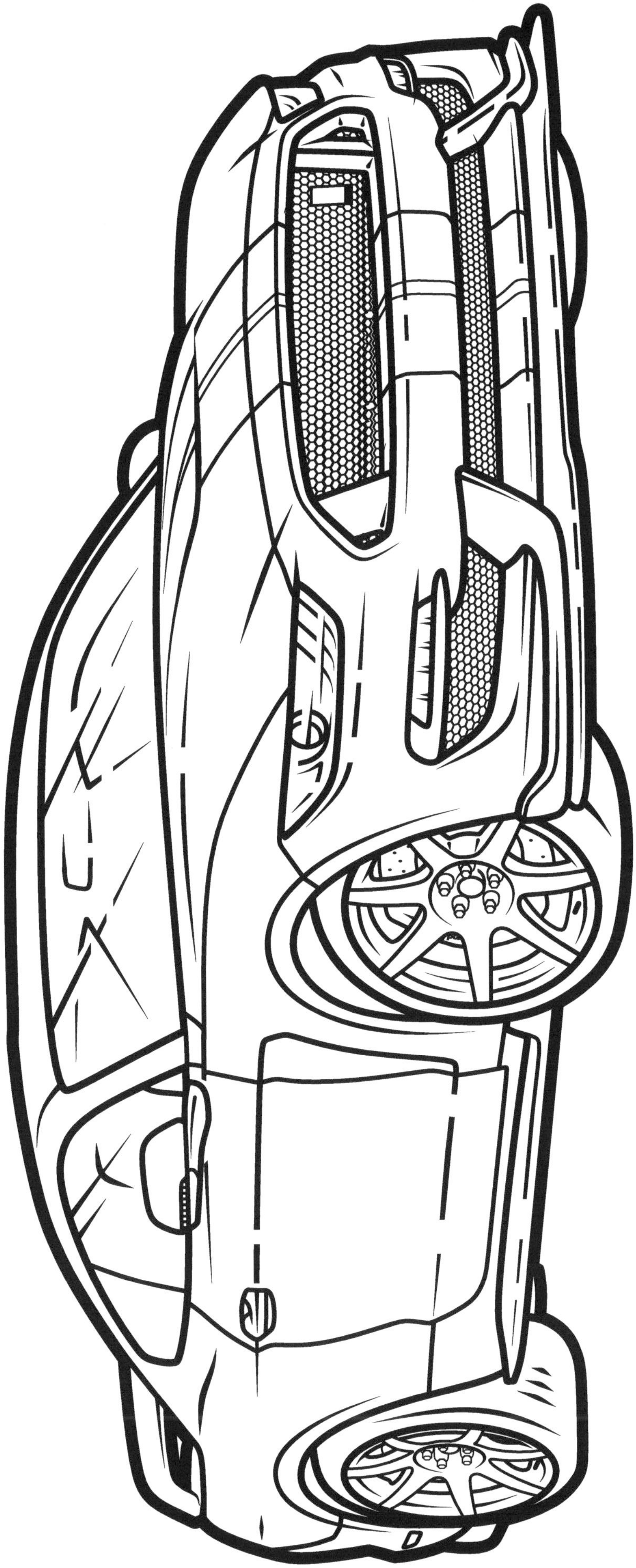

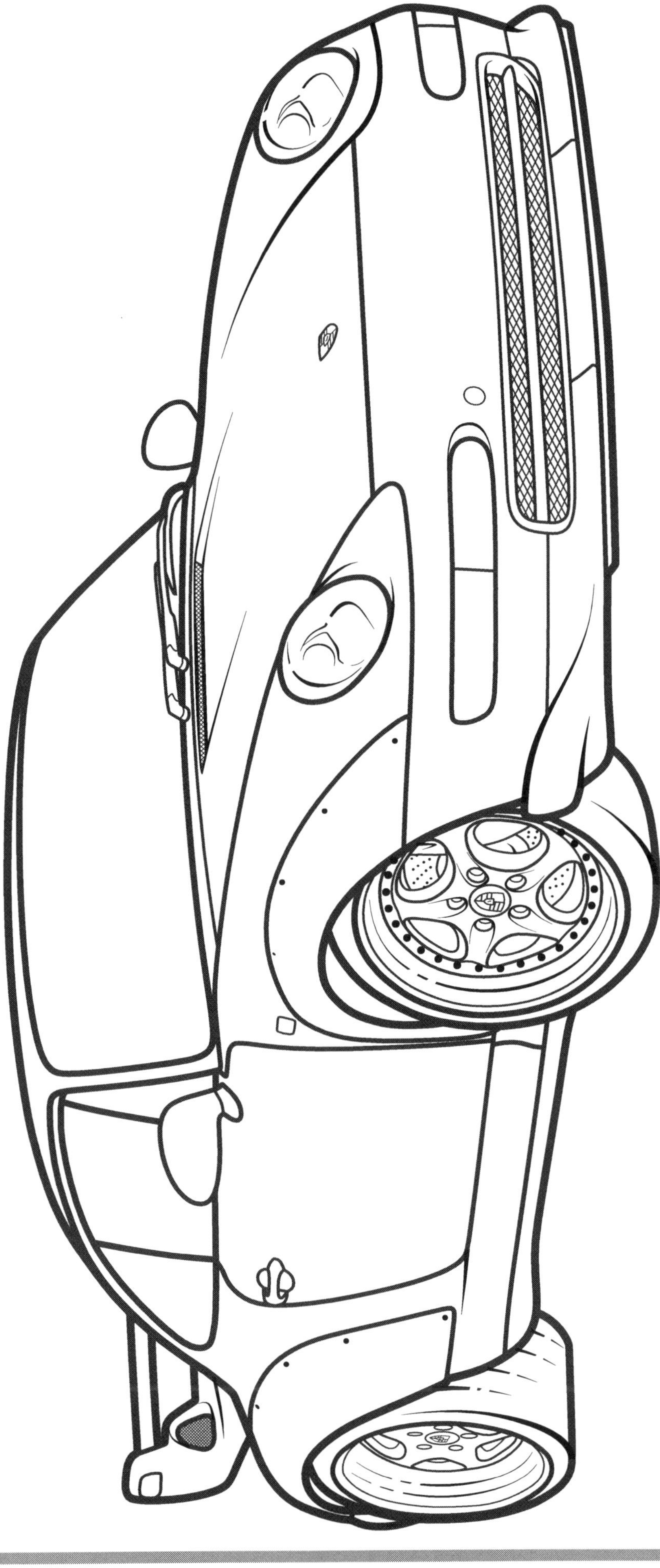

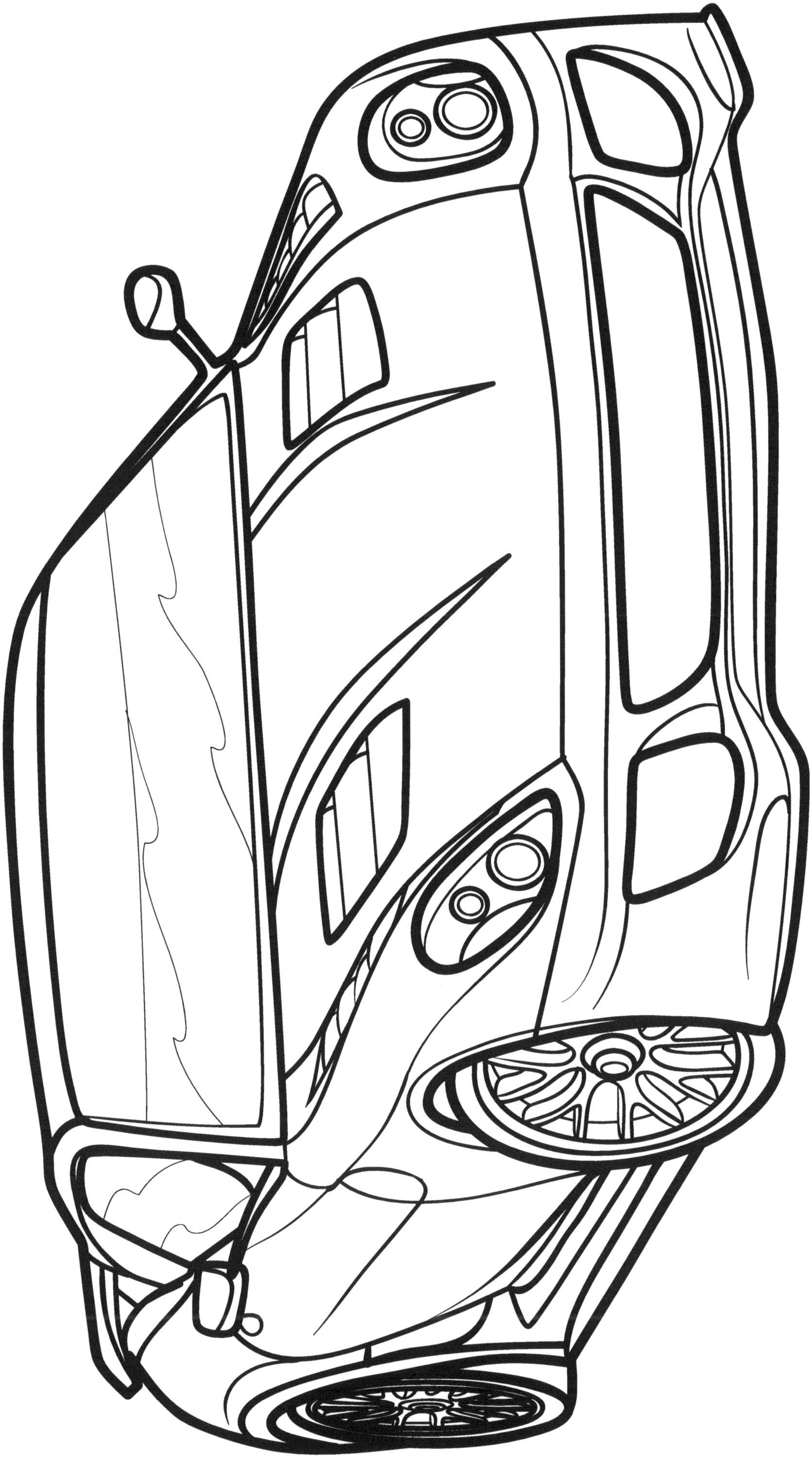

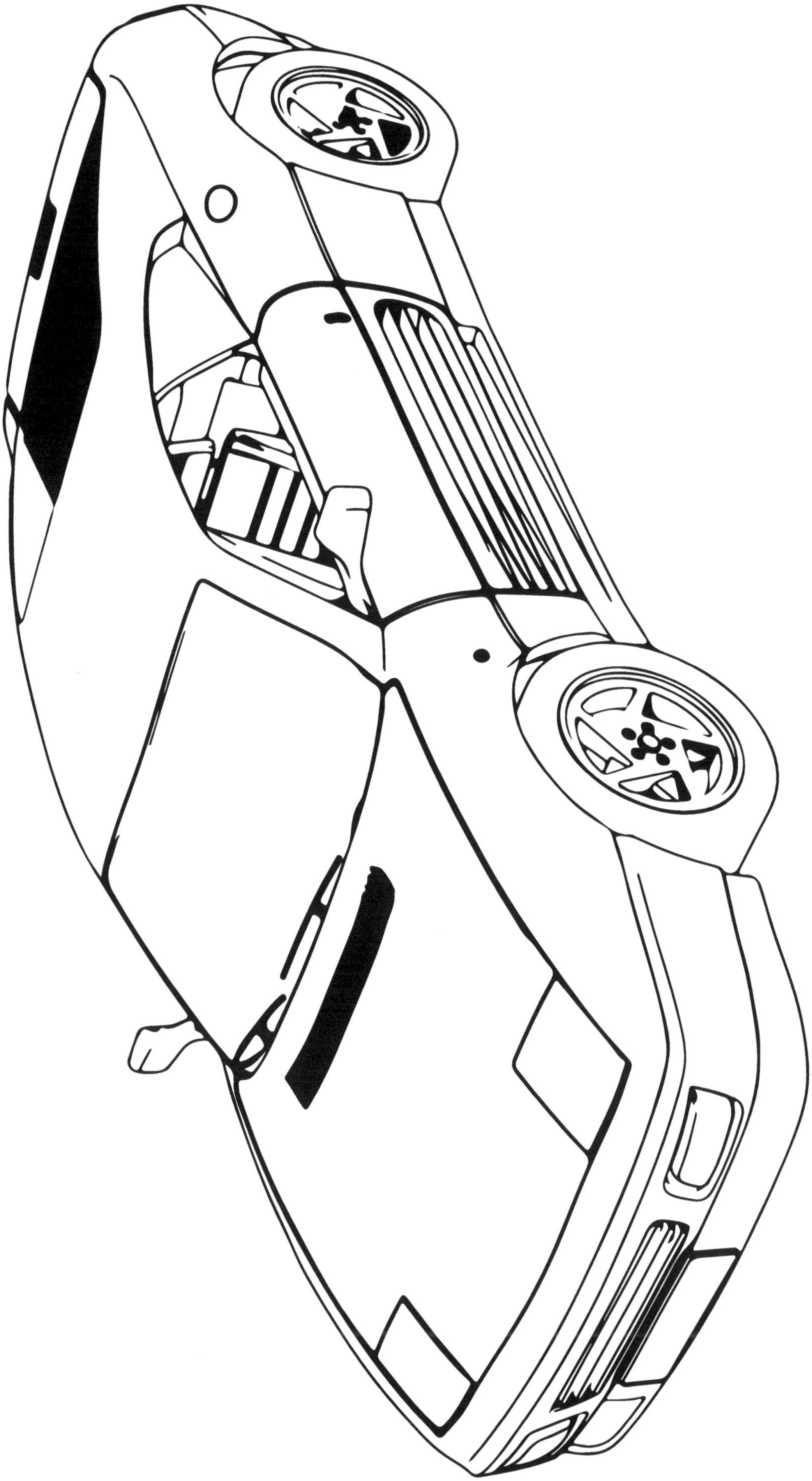

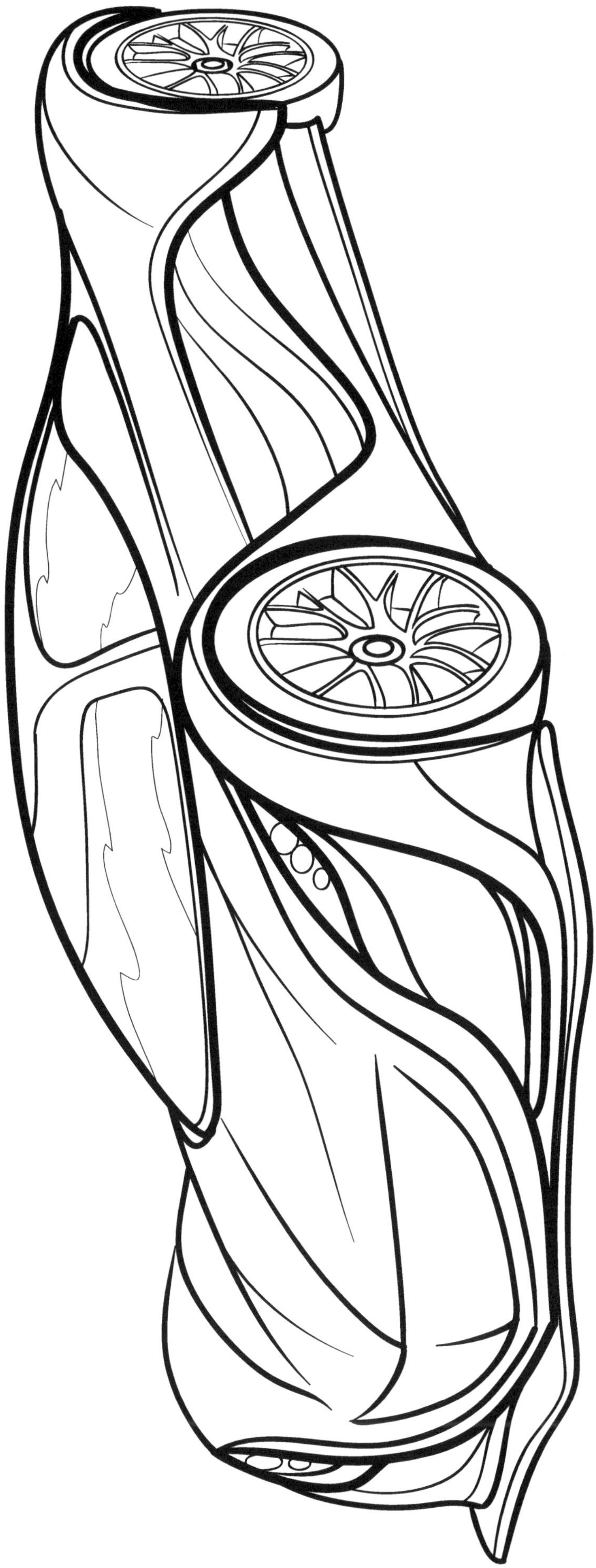

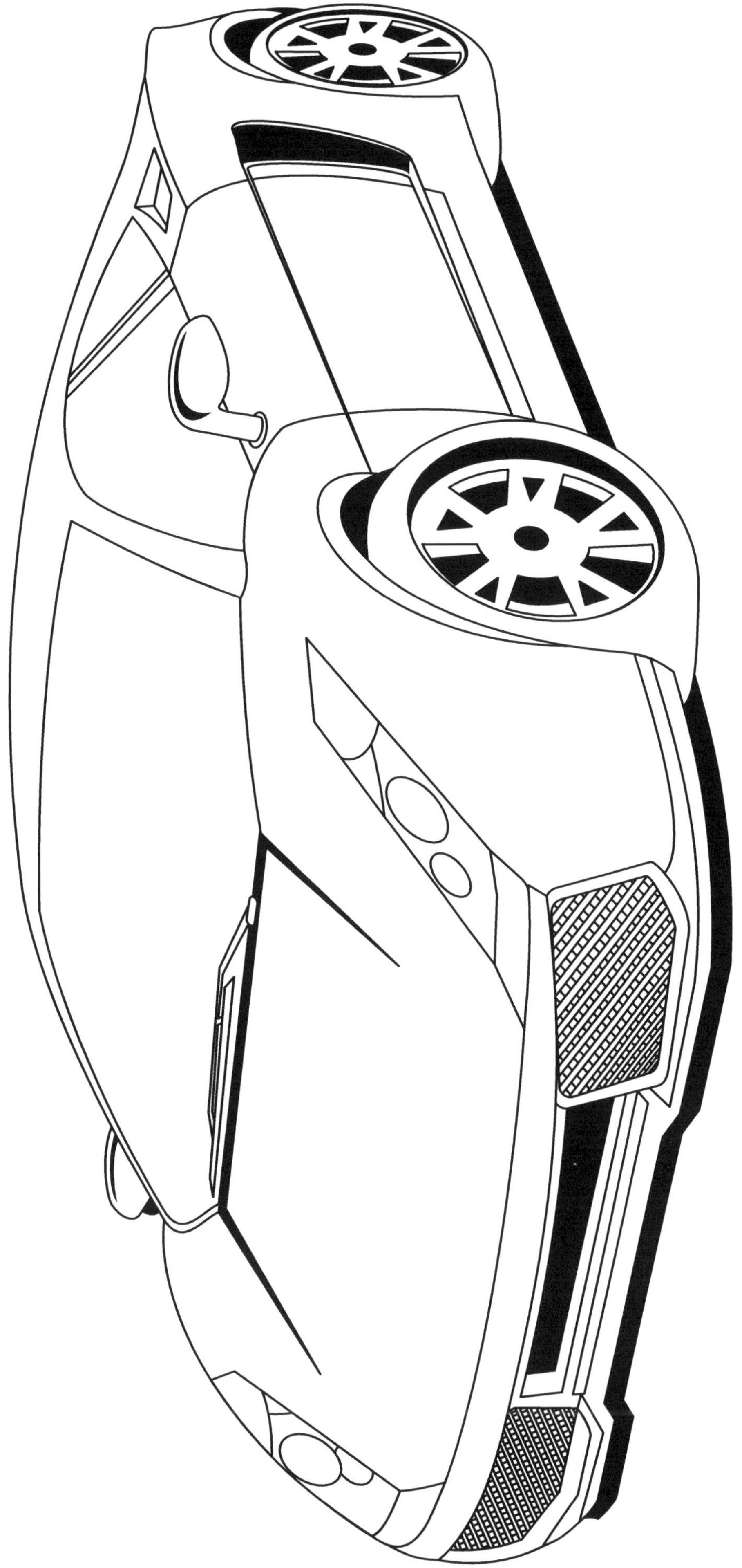

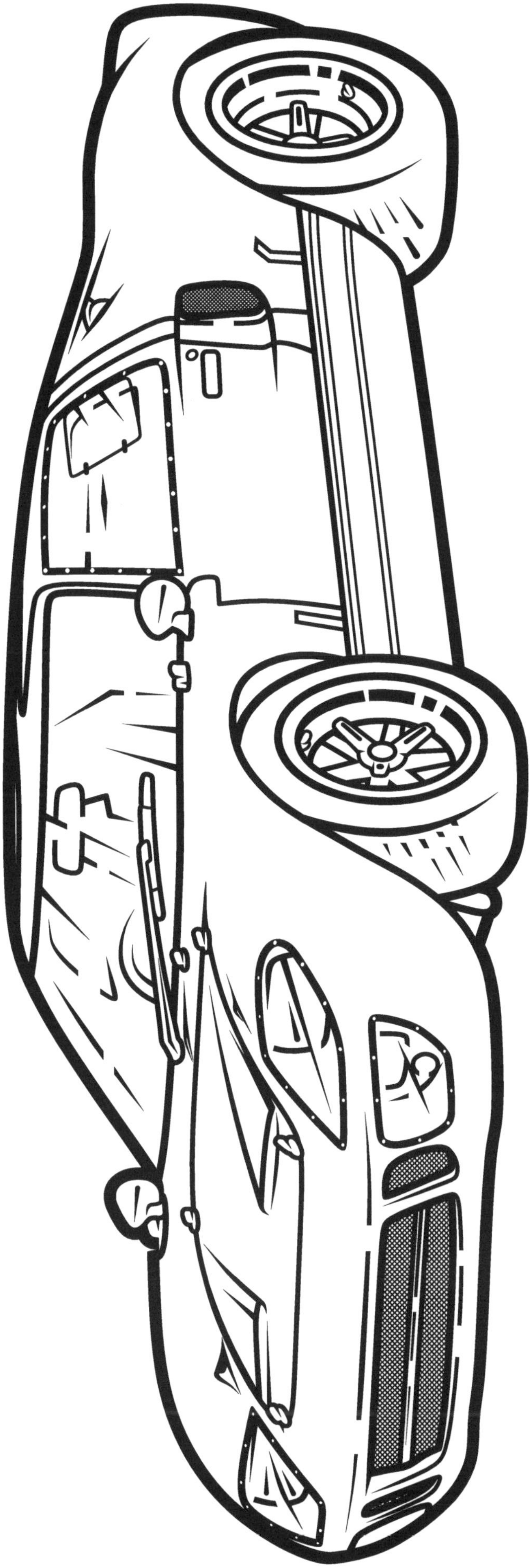

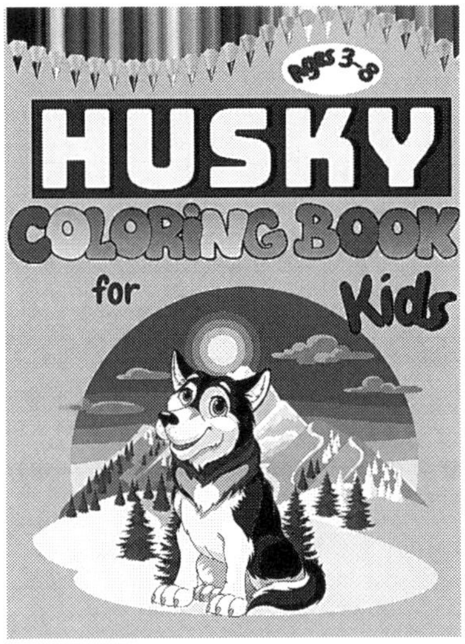

FOR MORE BOOKS
SCAN THE QR
CODE

Thank you!

inkHORSE Publishing